BYZANTIUM

BYZANTIUM
THE BRIDGE FROM ANTIQUITY
TO THE MIDDLE AGES

MICHAEL ANGOLD

St. Martin's Press   New York

www.stmartins.com

Library of Congress Cataloging-in-Publication Data

Angold, Michael.
    Byzantium: the bridge from antiquity to the Middle Ages / Michael Angold.
        p. cm.
    Includes bibliographical references and index.
    ISBN 0-312-28429-2
    1. Byzantine Empire—Civilization. I. Title.

DF521 .A55 2001
949.5'02—dc21   2001041619

First published in Great Britain by Weidenfeld & Nicolson

First U.S. Edition: November 2001

10 9 8 7 6 5 4 3 2 1

CONTENTS

ILLUSTRATIONS

The author and publishers would like to thank the following for permission to reproduce pictures: AKG, London, 7; AKG, London/ Erich Lessing, 14, 16; Ancient Art and Architecture Collection, 9, 10, 19, 26; Art Archive/Dagli Orti, 2, 3, 11, 12, 20, 32; Art Archive/Bibliothèque Nationale, Paris, 22; Bridgeman Art Library, 30; Lauros-Giraudon/Bridgeman Art Library, 23; Metropolitan Museum of Art, New York, 15; Werner Forman Archive, 27.

NOTES FOR TRAVELLERS

The events described in this book took place largely around the Mediterranean. The best time to travel is either the spring or the autumn. You can take your chances in March but it is often cold and rainy; April and May are better bets. The autumn is at its best in October, but, if you are lucky, an Indian summer may last well into November. The monuments of the early Middle Ages are widely scattered, but many of the best preserved and most evocative are concentrated in the cities of Rome, Ravenna, Thessaloniki, and Istanbul.

Byzantine civilization was far more original and creative than it is usually given credit for. Its domed churches challenge classical temples and Gothic cathedrals in their originality and daring, while its mosaics vie with classical sculpture and Renaissance painting as supreme works of art. Byzantine civilization was largely the creation of the city of Byzantium, or Constantinople, which is where we must begin. The massive and hugely impressive transformation that the city underwent in the centuries after 1453 – when it became Istanbul, the capital of the Ottoman Empire – did not obliterate the Byzantine city. How could it? Justinian's Church of St Sophia continues to preside. The nave with its colossal dome still staggers us. Much has been done to preserve what is left of the Byzantine mosaics. The apse mosaic of the Virgin and Child remains among the greatest works of Byzantine art. Within reasonably easy distance of St Sophia are other Justinianic churches. The Church of St Sergius and Bacchus (Küçük Ayasofya Camii) should not be missed for the daring of its planning and the beauty of its architectural detail. In contrast there is the Church of St Irene (Aya Irini Kilisesi), which impresses with its severity. Note the iconoclast cross in the apse. The church now stands within the precincts of the Topkapi Palace. This residence of the Ottoman sultans survives intact, which is more than can be said of the Byzantine imperial palace, which stood on the opposite side of St Sophia. More or less all that is left is a famous mosaic floor, which has been turned into the Mosaics Museum (Mozaik Müsesi), but archaeological work in the area promises to reveal more of the palace's splendours. Next to the palace was the hippodrome (At Meydani), where the chariot races were staged. It was in many ways the focus of city life. It is now a park, where some of the old monuments still stand, notably an Egyptian obelisk that the Byzantines mounted on a base showing scenes from the hippodrome. Even more evocative of the early Byzantine city are the public monuments. Close to St Sophia is the great Basilica cistern (Yerebatan Saray) built by Justinian. It was fed by water brought by the Aqueduct of Valens (Bozdogan Kemeri), which dwarfs Atatürk Bulvari, the main artery of the modern city. The walls of Constantinople should not be missed. Built in the early fifth century, they are the supreme achievement of Roman military engineering. It is worth making a special trip to the Sea of Marmora end in order to see the fortress of Yedikule, which contains the Golden Gate – now blocked up – the ceremonial entrance to the city of Constantinople. Within easy distance is the monastery of St John of Stoudios (Imrahor Camii). Though now just a shell, it was for a thousand years the greatest of Byzantine monasteries.

Ravenna and Thessaloniki complement early Constantinople. The former boasts the greatest surviving assemblage of sixth-century ecclesiastical buildings, and with most of their mosaic decoration still intact. There is San Vitale, with its famous mosaics of the courts of Justinian and Theodora and much more; San Appollinare Nuovo, with its processions of martyrs and virgins – don't miss the small portrait of Justinian as an old man hidden away at the west end; San Appollinare in Classe, with its lovely grey marble columns and its famous apse mosaic of the Transfiguration showing the apostles as sheep and Christ as a cross. There are the baptisteries and the mausoleum of Galla Placidia, with its star-spangled ceiling. Long stretches of the medieval walls are still intact. On Via di Roma next to San Appollinare Nuovo you can still make out the façade of the Byzantine governor's palace. Well worth the effort is the short trip out of town to the mausoleum of King Theodorich.

Thessaloniki doesn't have quite the same concentration of early medieval monuments, but there is the great pilgrimage Church of St Demetrius, still the city's focus, which dates back to the mid-fifth century. It has survived earthquakes and a succession of fires. Somehow it has still preserved some of its early medieval mosaic work. Within easy reach of St Demetrius are the Church of the Virgin Acheiropoieitos, an impressively large early Christian basilica; the Cathedral of St Sophia, built in the middle of the Dark Ages – clumsy but immensely solid with powerful mosaics in the apse and dome; and the Rotunda, a victim of the 1978 earthquake. The last has been restored and may soon open to the public. It was originally built around AD 300 as the mausoleum of the emperor Galerius – a notorious persecutor of Christians – but was later turned into a church, when the gold mosaics showing a calendar of saints were added. Tucked away among the winding lanes that lead up to the citadel is the tiny Church of Osios David, famed for its apse mosaic showing Christ in glory. It dates from the fifth century and is, if not the earliest, one of the earliest apse mosaics to have survived. A steep ascent will take you to the upper circuit of walls dating from roughly the same time.

It is quite impossible to do justice to Rome in a few words. The early medieval city is there, but you have to look for it, because it is obscured by later accretions. A marvellous exception are the ruins of Santa Maria Antiqua at the foot of the Palatine Hill. Its lavish frescoes give a taste of the richness of the early medieval decor. It has been preserved because it was overwhelmed by a mud slide in the ninth century, to be rediscovered a thousand years later. You are bound to visit the Pantheon, but reflect that its survival was the result of being turned into a Christian church, Santa Maria ad Martyres (Rotonda), which became one of the great pilgrimage churches of the Middle Ages. Pilgrims came to venerate an icon of the Virgin Mary donated by a Byzantine emperor in the early seventh century. Churches such as Santa Maria in Cosmedin and, particularly, San Prassede, which has been little altered, will give you a good impression of pilgrimage churches of the time. You should visit the crypts, where relics gathered from the catacombs were stored. But there is so much more.

You will find more early medieval sites and buildings scattered around Syria, Palestine, and Israel than anywhere else, but less easily accessible. There are desert palaces, deserted villages and market towns, and ruined cities boasting many churches. Not to be missed by anybody interested in early Islam are the Great Mosque at Damascus and the Dome of the Rock at Jerusalem. If you have the chance, visit the monastery of St Catherine at the foot of Mount Sinai. It was built by Emperor Justinian as a fortified monastery, and its original apse mosaic showing the Transfiguration has been preserved. It was an important place of pilgrimage, originally because of its associations with Moses, later because of the cult of St Catherine of Alexandria, famous for being broken on the wheel.

Norman Sicily gives us the opportunity to review the changes that occurred over the early Middle Ages. Most of the monuments are concentrated in and around the centre of Palermo. The Royal Palace is the place to start. Only one room from the Norman palace –

the Sala di Ruggero — has been preserved, but it is worth seeing. The palace chapel must not be missed. It combines Byzantine mosaics, Italian architecture and Muslim workmanship to create a dazzling ensemble. Don't miss the nearby ruined monastery of San Giovanni degli Eremiti. Down from the palace is the cathedral. It was built in the late twelfth century on the site of the chief mosque, but has since been much altered. It houses the porphyry tombs of the Norman kings and their successors. Continue down to the main street of Palermo (Via Maqueda). Immediately to your right is a square dominated by the churches of San Cataldo and Santa Maria dell' Ammiraglio (the Martorana). The former can be appreciated for its severe architecture, the latter for its campanile and its wonderful mosaics. Up from the Royal Palace, in the Piazza Independenza, you can catch a bus that will take you a short distance to La Cuba, one of the Moorish palaces of the Norman kings, and further afield up to Monreale — about half an hour by bus — and its stupendous cathedral. Amazingly, the original mosaic decoration is virtually intact. The cloister should not be missed. There is much else beside to see in and around Palermo, including a number of churches in the distinctive Norman Sicilian style. It is certainly worth making the effort to reach La Zisa, the most impressive and best preserved of the Moorish palaces of the Norman kings. But most of all Cefalù — about forty minutes by train from Palermo — must be seen: a delightful setting on the coast and a cathedral that somehow combines northern French architecture with Byzantine mosaics.

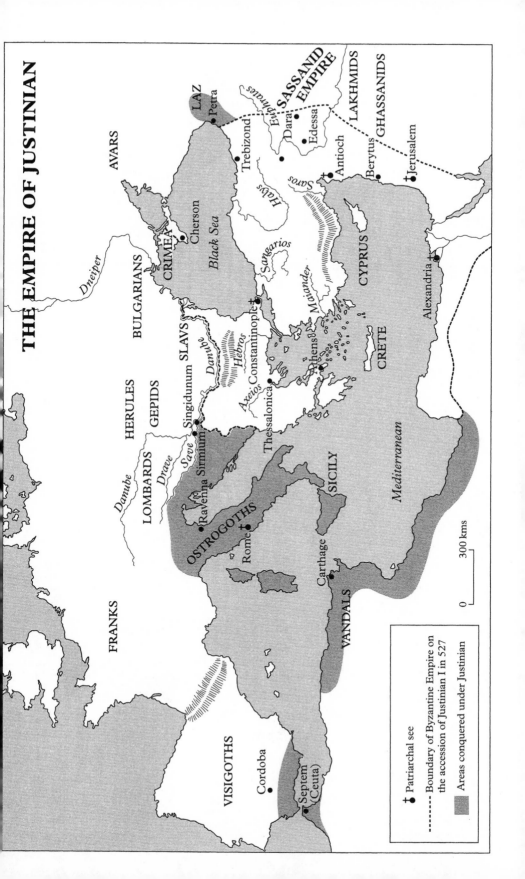

THE EMPIRE OF JUSTINIAN

FRANKS

VISIGOTHS

Cordoba •

Septem
(Ceuta) •

VANDALS

Carthage •

SICILY

Rome †

OSTROGOTHS

Ravenna •

Sirmium •

LOMBARDS

GEPIDS

HERULES

Danube

Drave

Save

Singidunum

SLAVS

BULGARIANS

AVARS

Dneiper

Thessalonica •

Axeios

Hebros

Danube

Constantinople †

Athens

Maiander

Sangarios

CRIMEA

Cherson •

Black Sea

Trebizond •

Halis

Saros

Saros

LAZ

Petra •

Euphrates

Dara •

Edessa •

**SASSANID
EMPIRE**

LAKHMIDS

Antioch †

Berytus •

GHASSANIDS

Jerusalem †

Mediterranean

CRETE

CYPRUS

Alexandria †

Legend:

† Patriarchal see

----- Boundary of Byzantine Empire on
the accession of Justinian I in 527

▓ Areas conquered under Justinian

0   300 kms

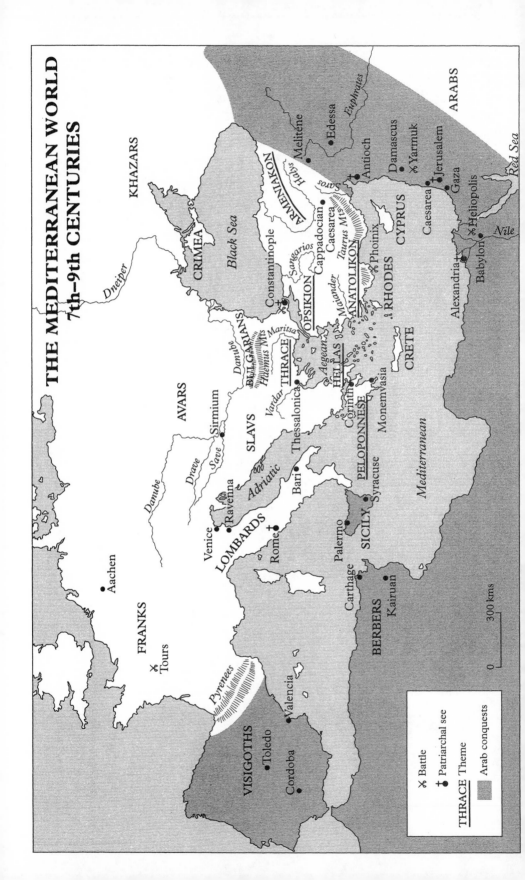

THE MEDITERRANEAN WORLD
7th–9th CENTURIES

KHAZARS

ARABS

Euphrates

• Melitēne
• Edessa

CRIMEA

Dneiper

Black Sea

ARMENIAKON

Halys

Antioch †
Damascus •
✗ Yarmuk
Jerusalem †
Gaza •
Heliopolis †
✗
Red Sea

Constantinople †

Sangarios

Cappadocian •
Caesarea •
Saros

CYPRUS

Caesarea •

Alexandria †
Babylon •
✗
Nile

OPSIKION

Taurus Mts

ANATOLIKON

✗ Phoinix

RHODES

BULGARIANS

Haemus Mts
Maritsa

THRACE

Maiander

Danube

Vardar

HELLAS

Aegean

CRETE

AVARS

SLAVS

Sirmium •

Save

Drave

Thessalonica •

Corinth •

PELOPONNESE

Monemvasia •

Danube

Ravenna

Venice •

Adriatic

Bari •

Palermo •
Syracuse •

SICILY

Mediterranean

LOMBARDS

Rome †

Carthage •

BERBERS

Kairuan •

FRANKS

✗ Tours

Aachen •

Pyrenees

VISIGOTHS

Toledo •
Cordoba •

Valencia •

✗ Battle
† Patriarchal see
THRACE Theme
▨ Arab conquests

0   300 kms

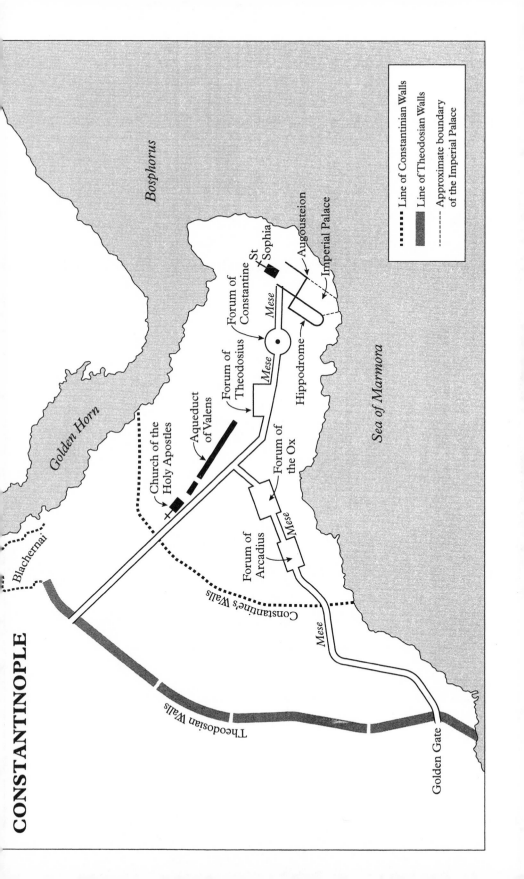

CONSTANTINOPLE

Bosphorus

Golden Horn

Sea of Marmora

Blachernai

Church of the Holy Apostles

Aqueduct of Valens

Forum of Theodosius

Forum of Constantine

St Sophia

Augousteion

Imperial Palace

Mese

Mese

Mese

Hippodrome

Forum of the Ox

Forum of Arcadius

Mese

Mese

Constantine's Walls

Theodosian Walls

Golden Gate

Line of Constantinian Walls
Line of Theodosian Walls
Approximate boundary
of the Imperial Palace

Chapter One

THE CITY OF CONSTANTINE

B yzantium in all its meanings is at the heart of this book. It holds the key to the development of the early medieval world, which saw unity give way to division; which saw Byzantium lose its cultural pre-eminence as it faced new rivals in the form of Islam and of the Latin West. In order to understand how Byzantium lost its cultural pre-eminence we must first trace how it obtained it. The starting point is the transformation of the classical world that prepared the way for the Middle Ages. Byzantium was the crucible and its development was therefore crucial.

Byzantium was an old Greek *polis*, or city-state, on the Bosphorus, never in antiquity of great significance. But this changed when Emperor Constantine the Great (306–37) refounded it as a new imperial capital in 324 and renamed it Constantinople – the city of Constantine – in his own honour. It was to serve as a new Rome, from which the Emperor could survey the most vulnerable frontiers of the empire, which stretched along the Danube and the Euphrates. The decision to site the centre of imperial authority on the banks of the Bosphorus had obvious implications for the relationship between the two halves of the empire. If in the end it pointed to division, it initially gave hope that the city might become a new focus of unity for the Roman world. This was the ideal that later

I

inspired Justinian I (527–65), but it was only ever realized in part. Instead of renewing unity, the transformation of the Roman order around Byzantium created a new entity, which it is appropriate to refer to as the Byzantine Empire. It is a usage that underlines that both empire and people were distinct from their Roman forerunners – it does not matter that the Byzantines almost always called it the Roman Empire and themselves Romans. The essence of the distinction between Roman and Byzantine is to be found in the capital city of Byzantium, where a new culture and political system were forged out of old materials.

The first and essential step was the foundation of a new capital. This was complemented by the work of Justinian, as both a legislator and a builder, symbolized by the Church of St Sophia, which set his indelible stamp upon Byzantium. The capital city and the civilization thus created derived added significance from the way they were seen as a thanks-offering to the Mother of God, who, it was fervently believed, safeguarded them. The Byzantines were the chosen people of the New Testament, the new Israelites; Constantinople was the God-guarded city, the new Jerusalem. Byzantine civilization was permeated with a belief in divine favour and vigilance. At its core was a process of reaction and interaction between capital, imperial office, and Christian church and faith. The patterns formed determined the shape taken by materials inherited from the Christian, Roman, and Hellenistic past: what would be selected or discarded, what combinations would be made. Byzantine civilization was imperial, Christian, and metropolitan.

But this civilization did not appear fully formed out of Constantine's head. He had done much to strengthen the Christian component within the Roman order in terms of both organization and material well-being, but at his death in 337 his achievement still seemed vulnerable. Christianity revealed a talent for dissension that persecution had concealed, and a reluctance to accept the full intimacy of the imperial embrace. Individuals can initiate drastic change, but it needs institutions – states or cities – to carry it through. It was Constantine's city that would bring his work of Christianizing the empire to a successful conclusion. However, when he died, his city was only half built; its forum and its arcaded streets hastily erected; its character still not clearly defined. It was his city, and it is conceivable that it could have died with him.

That it did not was the work of his son Constantius (337–61), who had been allotted Constantinople and the eastern provinces at his father's death. His two brothers received the western and central provinces of the empire respectively. It was a recipe for a series of civil wars, from which Constantius emerged victorious. His victory confirmed Constantinople as the imperial capital. Constantius enlarged on his father's plans for the city. He enhanced its claims to be the new Rome by giving it a senate on a par with that of Rome. He completed the Church of the Holy Apostles, which was his father's mausoleum. He emphasized the city's Christian character by building the first Church of St Sophia to serve as its cathedral. In 360 the city hosted a General Council of the Church convened by Constantius, who thus sought to elevate the church of Constantinople to patriarchal status. This proved premature because the council was later repudiated on the grounds that Constantius was using it to promote a form of the Arian doctrine, already condemned as heresy for impugning the full divinity of Christ.

Constantius's death in 361 was followed by a time of confusion, which threatened Constantinople's special position. Constantius was succeeded by his cousin Julian, a pagan, who hated the new Christian order symbolized for him by the lackeys of the imperial court at Constantinople. He found Antioch more to his taste, but he died in 363 on campaign against Persia, playing at being Alexander the Great. His death was followed by a division of the empire, with the eastern provinces eventually falling to Valens (364–78), who had no love of Constantinople either. He, too, made Antioch his headquarters, the better to survey the Persian frontier. It meant that he was out of touch with the situation along the Danube, where the sudden appearance of the Huns had panicked the Visigoths into seeking refuge on Roman soil. Their settlement was mismanaged. The Visigoths rebelled and caught Valens and his army at Adrianople in 378. The Emperor was killed. It was an utter disaster, which brought the Visigoths to within striking distance of Constantinople and threatened its claims to be the imperial capital.

But the work of Constantius had not been in vain. It provided a basis on which the man sent from the West to rescue the situation could work. His name was Theodosius (379–95). He was of Spanish origin, a good general, and a devout Catholic. His first move once he had contained the Visigothic threat was to call a General Council of the Church to Constantinople in 381. Its major purpose was to confirm that the Catholic brand of Christianity was the accepted orthodoxy. The Arian form was outlawed and Theodosius then enacted a law that made the new orthodoxy the religion of the Roman Empire. *Civis romanus* and *Christianus catholicus* were thenceforward interchangeable. But the council of 381 did other things beside imposing Catholicism on the church universal. It effectively raised the church of Constantinople to patriarchal status. It was given the same rank as the church of Jerusalem, underlining that Constantinople was not only the new Rome, but also the new Jerusalem. Despite its lack of apostolic origins – these would have to be manufactured in the shape of the legend of St Andrew – Constantinople ranked as one of the major centres of Christianity.

Theodosius did more than ensure that Constantinople's church had patriarchal status. He resumed the work of construction, which had been more or less left in abeyance since the death of Constantius twenty years earlier. Like Constantine, he built himself a forum. This was opened up along the 'Imperial Avenue', the Mese, some quarter of a mile to the east of Constantine's forum. It was embellished with a great triumphal archway. In the centre of the forum was a huge column, on the summit of which was placed a silver statue of Theodosius. Another way of setting his stamp on Constantinople was by enlarging the hippodrome, where emperor and citizens were united in the enjoyment of chariot racing. Theodosius had an obelisk brought from Karnak in Egypt and set it up along the central ridge, the *spina*, of the hippodrome. He had the base of the obelisk decorated with various scenes, such as the emperor and his family watching the racing at the hippodrome from the imperial box and receiving tribute from defeated peoples. The hippodrome provided a stage on which the ties binding the emperor and his people could be continually renewed: standing in the imperial box the emperor would present himself to the people and receive their acclamations. The people's role was not entirely passive, for the emperor might have to stand and listen to an account of their grievances, which it was unwise to ignore. It would take time for the relationship of emperor and people of Constantinople to be clarified, but by drawing attention to the importance of the hippodrome Theodosius helped to initiate the process by which the imperial office came to be rooted in the society of the capital.

Under Theodosius's patronage a new period of growth began. A court orator of the time noted that the built-up area within the walls was beginning to exceed the open spaces, and land started to be reclaimed from the sea for building purposes. At last, in 412, the government of Theodosius's grandson and namesake built a line of walls, which still stands, nearly a mile west of Constantine's walls. Perhaps a third was added to the area of the city. A contemporary noted that the population of the new Rome was now beginning to outstrip that of the old. We can therefore think in terms of a population of at least quarter of a million.

THE CITY TAKES SHAPE

Constantinople was beginning to assume its distinctive shape. It was articulated by two main avenues. Starting from the Golden Gate, the ceremonial entrance into the city near the northern end of the Theodosian Walls, and the Charisian Gate, near the southerly end, they met at the Forum of Theodosius and proceeded eastwards through the Forum of Constantine to the Augustaion. This square was the heart of the empire. It was dominated by a huge porphyry column bearing a statue of the Augusta: Emperor Constantine's mother, St Helena, the discoverer of the true cross. At its entrance stood the *milion*, or milepost. It was in the form of a triumphal arch and from it were measured the distances to all points within the empire. All roads now led to the new Rome, as was emphasized by the world map set up at the *milion* on the orders of Theodosius II (408–50). Arranged around the Augustaion were the Cathedral of St Sophia; the senate house; the Chalke, or Brazen, Gate, the ceremonial entry into the imperial palace; and, near the entrance, the hippodrome. All the major institutions of the Empire were housed around the square. Official visitors to Constantinople would travel up the great avenue of the Mese, which opened up at intervals into huge squares, until they found themselves, after a journey of nearly three miles, entering the final sanctum of the Augustaion. It was immensely impressive, even in the declining years of the empire, when the great monuments were in ruins and large sections of the city abandoned. But in the fifth century, when all was pristine, the effect must have been overwhelming. If you try to recreate the city of Constantinople in your mind's eye, the great public squares, with their columns, statues, triumphal arches, and arcades, would appear like some fantastic neo-classical townscape.

Features of Constantinople were its shopping arcades and monumental stairways. An official inventory of the monuments of the city drawn up in the early fifth century lists no fewer than 52 arcades and 117 stairways. The configuration of Constantinople – a central ridge sloping sharply down to water on both sides – demanded stairways leading from one level to another. Their importance to the life of the city was underlined by the fact that they were the point of distribution of the corn dole: this consisted of a daily ration of six loaves of bread to which each free citizen was entitled. Apart from the main avenues, the public squares, the shopping arcades, and the monumental stairways, there was little in the way of planning. There was a marked contrast between the order that characterized the public or ceremonial face of the city and the lack of order evident in private development. Churches, mansions, tenement blocks, and shops were built haphazardly in a maze of alleys that led off the main thoroughfares. Laws prohibiting the construction of private buildings in public spaces or regulating the permissible height of tenements and the permissible distance between them somehow underline the chaotic development of a great city, which by the early fifth century was growing organically; it was no longer the artificial creation of a great emperor.

Constantinople was a city of quarters. These sprang up very rapidly from the time of Theodosius I. A surprising number of them took their name from men who had been prominent in the government of Theodosius I and of his son and grandson. The origin of these quarters is probably to be found in property belonging to the people in question. It may have been a matter of turning land to profit by building on it, but it is more likely that these quarters came into being around the residences of these great families. We can obtain an idea of what these were like from an inventory from about the year 400 of the property belonging to the heiress of one of the most influential families of the day. Her name was Olympias and she was the granddaughter of a trusted minister of Emperor Constantius. She inherited estates near Constantinople, as well as others scattered over Thrace and Anatolia, which provided her with the bulk of her income and which she administered from her residence near the Church of the Holy Apostles in Constantinople. She also possessed another complex of property in the capital close to the Church of St Sophia. It consisted not only of a residence with private baths and a bakery, but also of the surrounding buildings, which were rented out as workshops, shops, and accommodation. Much of the activity of the area would be directed towards supplying the needs of this residence. There is one telling detail that suggests that the inhabitants of the place looked towards Olympias as a patron: she disposed of a number of shares in the corn dole, which, with the passage of time, had come increasingly under the control of the rich and powerful. It points to the ties of clientage as a feature of the creation of new quarters. In this particular case, the complex was used by Olympias to found a convent, which explains how in some instances monastic foundations stood at the centre of various quarters. Another good example is the monastery of St John Stoudios, which still stands in a ruinous state not far from the Golden Gate. It was founded in the middle of the fifth century by Stoudios, a man important enough to have been consul.

From the reign of Theodosius monasteries played a considerable role in creating the fabric of the city. Monks and monasteries would become a feature of the medieval Christian city, but Constantinople seems in this regard to have anticipated developments. The early monks at Constantinople were inspired by an ideal that set them apart from the monks of the Egyptian desert: they did not wish to lead lives that separated them from everyday life; instead, they aimed to keep alive the Christian ethic within secular society. The most practical way that this could be done was through works of charity. This ideal helped to mould the character of monasticism at Constantinople. Though very often founded by the rich and powerful, the monasteries of the capital ministered to the needs of the poor and remained agents of the Christian ideal of charity. Their work helped towards the stabilization of society at a time of rapid expansion, when immigrants were pouring into the city from the provinces. It was 'a city in Thrace that grows rich from the sweat of the provinces', according to a contemporary from Antioch. Through the monasteries a proportion of the wealth of the great families was diverted to welfare purposes. The monasteries had, from the beginning, a central role at Constantinople as mediators between the rich and poor. The monks were always a powerful force within the capital, capable of opposing emperors and challenging patriarchs. They were integral to the growth of a new Christian capital, where imperial authority acquired a richer and more complicated character by association with a living society.

The creation of a new capital reversed the trends set in motion from the third century by imperial neglect of Rome. The progressive abandonment of Rome as the imperial centre of operations had meant that the official culture of the late Roman Empire lost definition and became more abstruse. The effects are obvious in the imperial art of the time, which sought to divorce imperial authority from place and time. Without a proper capital, imperial authority lost contact with reality. This contact was progressively restored from the turn of the fourth century, as imperial authority became rooted once again in a new capital city, but one that was fervently Christian. It dramatized one major problem: how would Christianity alter the quality of imperial authority?

RELIGION AND POLITICS

Roman emperors had increasingly adopted the Hellenistic notion that the emperor participated in the divine. He was the point of intersection between the supreme deity and Roman society. Conversion to Christianity required certain modifications. Constantine the Great had to define his position more clearly. He claimed to be the 'equal of the Apostles' and the 'friend of Jesus Christ'. He wanted to inject a personal dimension into his relationship with Christ. Some scholars have detected an element of self-identification. Certainly, there was something scandalous about Constantine's plan for his mausoleum at the Church of the Holy Apostles, where he would have been buried surrounded by relics of the Apostles. A claim to his semi-divine status helps to explain the opposition he had to confront from within the church. This was led by Athanasius, the patriarch of Alexandria (328–73). Athanasius was a champion of the autonomy of the church and resented what he saw as imperial interference in its affairs. He was sent into exile, but continued his opposition under Constantine's successors, on the grounds that they had adopted Arianism, a heretical form of Christianity that Constantine had been toying with in his last years. Theodosius I abandoned his predecessors' religious stance and accepted the orthodox, or Catholic, line that had been upheld by Athanasius. He learnt to his cost what this meant when he was refused communion for actions that were seen as prejudicial to the church. Perhaps most cuttingly of all, Ambrose, Bishop of Milan, refused him communion after the Emperor had won a great battle, which delivered the Western Empire from a paganizing regime. The Bishop argued that the Emperor must atone for the human blood he had spilt. It was a demonstration that not even an emperor was immune to the moral authority and powers of discipline exercised by the church, and it was a humiliation that hastened Theodosius's death a few months later.

The relationship of imperial and spiritual authority was always going to be intractable. Theodosius's experience suggested that the imperial office was now subject to the moral and spiritual supervision of the church and could no longer claim to be in direct contact with the divine. For a moment it seemed as though the Emperor was likely to lose all initiative in ecclesiastical affairs. If this did not happen, it was a result of the alliance that developed between the Emperor and his patriarch at Constantinople. It was not quite as simple as the patriarch acting as the Emperor's agent in religious affairs or the Emperor acting as the patriarch's protector. There was always an element of trial and error in the relationship between emperor and patriarch, and in the early fifth century it still had to be worked out. The patriarchate of John Chrysostom (398–404) was critical in this respect. It established a pattern of cooperation, conflict, and recrimination.

Chrysostom was a charismatic figure, the greatest preacher of his age. His hold on the capital was confirmed when, in 399, he roused its populace against the Gothic mercenaries who were quartered in Constantinople. He objected to them because they followed the Arian form of Christianity. Their presence was an insult to orthodoxy. It was the duty of the people to rise up and drive them out, which they did. This was the first demonstration of a feature of the history of Constantinople: the close connection of religion and politics. This was not the only way in which Chrysostom pointed the way forward. The claims of his church to patriarchal status had emerged from the Council of 381, but the privileges it received were still largely honorific. It was Chrysostom who set about transforming them into something more concrete. He extended the jurisdiction of his church into Thrace and Anatolia. He also tried to build up its financial strength by seeking to gain control of the wealthy charitable institutions of the city. This earned him the enmity of the monks who staffed these places. Brought up in the ascetic tradition of Syrian monasticism, Chrysostom thought the activities of the monks of Constantinople a perversion of the monastic ideal. He wanted them driven from the city. The outcome of this struggle underlined that the monks represented an independent force in the life of the capital.

The starting point was a dispute within the patriarchate of Alexandria that was laid before Emperor Arcadius (395–408). The Emperor sent it to Chrysostom for a decision. Arcadius seemed to be assuming that the church of the imperial capital was becoming a court of appeal for cases coming from other Churches. The implication was that the church of Constantinople was claiming a primacy of jurisdiction over the church at large. Chrysostom defied imperial wishes and very properly declined the commission on the grounds that he would be exceeding his powers. He immediately forfeited the support of the imperial court, which saw his action as a betrayal of trust.

Thanks to the support of the monks, the imperial will prevailed. The monks were now instrumental in having Chrysostom removed from office. They drove him into exile – a drama made all the more intense by the destruction of St Sophia, which was burnt to the ground. Chrysostom's short patriarchate of only six years anticipated nearly every aspect of church–state relations at Byzantium. It was a dynamic, often explosive, relationship, which involved both the people and the monks of the capital. However, the stormy scenes surrounding Chrysostom's deposition revealed the dangers of a confrontation between emperor and patriarch, and underlined how necessary their cooperation was for proper imperial government. This became central to the ideology of a Christian Roman Empire, which was still in the process of being fully worked out. An important step was taken in 415, when emperor and patriarch joined together to reconsecrate the newly rebuilt Church of St Sophia.

There were, and continued to be, many contradictions in the idea of a Christian Empire. These were eased by the way the emperor showed a different face according to the setting. In the patriarchal Church of St Sophia the emperor and patriarch recognized their mutual obligations. The secular side of imperial authority was on display in the hippodrome, where the emperor was united with his people in victory celebrations. In the imperial palace he was the embodiment of earthly majesty, the law incarnate, the heir of Emperor Augustus, but also the legatee of Constantine's conversion to Christianity. It was here that the emperor was most obviously the Christian God's vicegerent on earth. The imperial palace of Constantinople therefore received a special Christian imprint. Under Emperor Theodosius II (408–50) it would start to become a treasure house of relics. The moving spirit was the Emperor's pious sister, Pulcheria. She brought Constantine's Cross into the palace as a palladium of victory, and had the relics of St Stephen laid to rest in a chapel that she had specially constructed. Turning the imperial palace into a Christian shrine was a way of adapting imperial authority to Christian susceptibilities.

Imperial art derived its power in large measure from ceremonial, which supplied meaning and context. It could also freeze imperial authority at a significant moment. In this way art could be used to disseminate imperial authority to the ends of the empire. Imperial portraits were set up in public places throughout the empire, and it was normal to pay the same honours to the imperial image as to the imperial person. Art was used to focus and convey imperial power. It was a means of communicating the complicated imperial ideology that stressed divine approval.

The citizens of Constantinople gloried in the magnificence of the imperial palace, which was a token of divine favour. This was at the heart of that identification of empire and capital that was so important an aspect of Byzantine ideology. It fed the citizens' sense of self-importance and was the cause of some resentment elsewhere. It raised the question of the new capital's status in relation not only to the empire, but also to the church at large. The old established centres of Christianity, such as Antioch, Alexandria, and Rome, saw the church of Constantinople potentially as an instrument for imperial control of the church universal. Its prestige was for the moment limited by its lack of good apostolic origins and by its failure to develop any distinct doctrinal position, in contrast to Alexandria, Antioch, and Rome, in the so-called Christological dispute. This centred on the question of how the divine and human natures of Christ related. Alexandria favoured a Monophysite solution, which argued that Christ's natures fused into a single nature. Rome and Antioch wished to maintain a distinction, so that Christ's humanity was not swallowed up in his divinity. The church of Constantinople found itself caught in the middle. In theological terms it counted for very little in comparison with Rome and

Alexandria. In 451 Pope Leo I (440–61) was able to bring the full influence of Rome to bear in order to persuade the court of Constantinople to convene another General Council of the Church to settle the matter. It was held at Chalcedon, just across the Bosphorus from Constantinople. Christ, it was decided this time, was 'in two natures, distinct but inseparable': perfect man and perfect God. This accorded with the teaching of Pope Leo and was a victory for Rome.

Chalcedon solved very little in the long run. It is easy to trace back to these disputes of the early fifth century the later divisions of the medieval world. The West, under Rome's leadership, seemed to be assuming a particular religious identity; equally so the eastern provinces under Alexandria. As yet, Constantinople had no distinctive voice. It was instead developing a distinctive function. Its role was to conciliate; to promote ecclesiastical unity as an essential foundation of imperial authority. It seems somehow appropriate that the patriarchs of Constantinople assumed the title of ecumenical patriarch.

By the middle of the fifth century Constantinople had emerged as a great city, in terms of size and influence probably the most powerful centre of the Roman world. Remembering that a century and a half earlier it was an obscure city in Thrace, its emergence as the imperial capital was in all sorts of ways unsettling. It was an artificial creation. It was only at the turn of the fourth century that it had acquired an existence of its own, based on a combination of organic growth and an ideological role. It began to develop a dynamism that was capable of transforming the Roman order, although the nature and extent of this transformation were still far from clear. The ideal was to preserve the unity of the Roman world around this new capital, but, in the face of ecclesiastical divisions and the fall of the Western Empire to the barbarian, it seemed that Constantinople might not have the power and resources to achieve this. Despite the work of Theodosius I and his successors, the legacy of Constantine was still vulnerable. It is possible by the middle of the fifth century to glimpse the lineaments of Byzantium, but they still lack clear definition.

Chapter Two

BYZANTIUM

T he creation of an imperial capital at Constantinople in the course of the fourth and early fifth centuries had a colossal impact. It mobilized the resources of the surrounding swathe of lands from the coasts of the Aegean to the shores of the Black Sea. Despite the presence of the great 'university' town of Athens, this region had been a backwater under the Roman Empire, part of the corridor linking its eastern and western parts. These lands were now the fulcrum of the whole empire, its most important parts in terms of wealth and population. The provincial cities prospered as dependants of the new imperial capital.

POWER SHIFTS TO THE EAST

The foundation and growth of Constantinople entirely altered the balance of the Roman Empire: its centre of gravity shifted to the East. The West was left open to barbarian conquest, which was all the more of an insult because the German conquerors adopted the heretical Arian form of Christianity. The emperors at Constantinople initially fulfilled their responsibilities to go to the help of the West. This culminated in the great expedition that Emperor Leo I (457–74) launched in 468 against North Africa in an effort to wrest it from the Vandals. At the same time he dispatched another army to Italy with the aim of putting an Eastern candidate on the Western throne. This effort to recover the Western Empire anticipated the plans of Justinian, but was an utter disaster. Leo's successors abandoned the West to its fate. The imperial government in Constantinople cut its losses and recognized the authority of the barbarian leaders who controlled Italy. Even the ecclesiastical links were, to all intents and purposes, severed.

The creed agreed at Chalcedon in 451 owed much to the formulations of Pope Leo I. It was not, however, acceptable to the bulk of the population of the Eastern provinces, where opinion favoured a Monophysite interpretation, emphasizing the divinity of Christ. The imperial government had no wish to call another General Council of the Church to decide the matter. Chalcedon had certain advantages. It presented a compromise theology and confirmed the church of Constantinople's claims to patriarchal status. It was, in any case, the emperor's responsibility to put into practice the decisions reached at a General Council. The result was an imperial edict of 484, known as the *Henotikon*. This did not abrogate the canons promulgated at Chalcedon. It accepted that Christ was perfect man and perfect God but insisted that there was a level – far beyond human understanding – where the divine and human elements within Christ fused. The papacy understood this to be directed against Pope Leo I and a state of schism ensued.

When the Emperor Anastasius (491–518) ascended the throne of Constantinople, he found that he ruled over a church and empire that were confined to the eastern provinces. The West had been jettisoned. This does not mean that a 'Byzantine' Empire was therefore in existence. The empire over which Anastasius presided was curiously unsatisfactory. Because he left behind the largest treasure ever recorded by a Roman emperor, he has gone down in history as a great ruler. His reign was, in fact, exceedingly troubled. The most serious opposition came from within his capital and can be seen as the continuing birthpangs of Byzantium. The patriarch of Constantinople opposed his accession and insisted that as the price of his coronation he make a profession of faith, which confirmed that in matters of faith and conduct the emperor came under the surveillance not just of the church, but specifically of the patriarch of Constantinople. It gave a new twist to a relationship that was at the heart of Byzantium. Anastasius was in a difficult position. He was a convinced Monophysite; the patriarch of Constantinople was an adherent of Chalcedon. The population of the capital was split, with a large Latin-speaking element that tended to favour Rome. In 511 Anastasius deposed the patriarch and replaced him with a more flexible cleric, who made the following concession to the Emperor's religious sympathies: he allowed the addition of the Monophysite slogan 'who was crucified for us' to the processional chant known as the *trisagion*: 'Holy God, holy and mighty, holy and immortal, have mercy on us.' This led to rioting on the streets of Constantinople. Anastasius was now aged over eighty. He appeared before the populace in the hippodrome and offered to resign the throne in the face of popular displeasure. The people were taken in by this display of humility and acclaimed him anew. As they left, the Emperor sent in his guards to massacre them. Even if the incident ended in the way it did, it was proof of the power of popular opinion.

The massacre did not put an end to popular disturbances, which had now become self-generating because of the activities of the circus factions – the Blues and the Greens. These factions, which were to be a characteristic feature of Byzantine public life until 1204, were originally an import from Rome, part of the way the new Rome was equipped with the institutions of the old. The hippodrome was the main gathering place of the capital and the factions were responsible for organizing the races and other activities that went on there. They were also involved in the acclamation of a new emperor after the ceremonial of the elevation to the imperial office was transferred to the hippodrome in the mid-fifth century. This gave their actions a political character that had previously been lacking, and emperors paid more attention to the circus factions as the fifth century wore on. As a gesture, Anastasius had the imperial box at the hippodrome decorated with portraits of famous charioteers of the day. His favourite was a Libyan called Porphyrius, to whom he set up at least two statues. They were partly in recognition of his sporting prowess, but also a mark of gratitude for the way that the charioteer had, at the head of the Greens, helped to defend the Emperor against the claims of a rival.

The irruption of the factions into the political life of Constantinople added a thoroughly anarchic element. The factions did not have any clear-cut religious or political programme beyond the protection of their privileges, but their support was worth cultivating, as Anastasius proved. The social composition of the factions was identical: their leaders and patrons came from the upper ranks of society; their activists were drawn from the young of all sections of society, who followed their leaders of the moment. Faction members affected particular styles: they grew their beards and moustaches long in the Persian manner; they copied the wild nomads of the steppes by letting their hair grow down at the back like a mane, while cutting it short at the front. They wore capes and trousers in the barbarian fashion, and a tunic gathered very tight at the wrists with billowing sleeves and exaggeratedly broad shoulders. They purposely adopted a style of dress and coiffure that set them apart from the rest of society. Their loyalties were passionate, cutting across any other conceivable social tie, but the basis of these loyalties is only occasionally revealed.

In the case of Theodora, who became Justinian's empress, it was bitter experience. She came from a family that worked for the Greens. Her father was their bearkeeper. He died when Theodora was still a child; his wife married again, but her new husband was not made bearkeeper of the Greens, not even when Theodora went with her sisters into the hippodrome as suppliants before the assembled faction. Theodora was turned into a lifelong and venomous opponent of the Greens. She attached herself to the Blues and thus obtained the introduction she craved to a patron of that faction. He was Justinian, a nephew of Justin I (518–27), who had secured the imperial dignity on the death of Anastasius.

Justin was a Latin-speaker from the heart of the Balkans. As a young man he had walked to Constantinople and had enrolled in the palace guard. He rose to the influential position of count of the excubitores, which put him in charge of palace security. While he was a man of no education, scarcely able to sign his name, he made sure that his nephew Justinian obtained an excellent education. Justinian repaid his uncle by masterminding the coup that brought him to the throne. The details are complicated but the drama was played out in the hippodrome. Justinian was able to bribe the circus factions to acclaim his uncle emperor rather than any of the other candidates. It was an episode that underlined the power of the circus factions.

It also underlined how unsatisfactory Anastasius's style of rule had been. 'Autocracy tempered by assassination' is a favourite way of describing the Byzantine constitution, but it is rather far from the mark. Succession at Byzantium was orderly more often than not, and, broadly speaking, dynastic. Anastasius may not have left any heirs of his body, but he had nephews, one of whom would in the normal course of events have been expected to succeed, in the same way that Justinian would succeed his uncle. Anastasius's failure was to provide clear direction. Tolerance and compromise are admirable from today's standpoint; they were not thus regarded in Anastasius's day. The imperial policy of disregarding Chalcedon meant a lack of clarity on central issues of dogma. Abandoning Rome and the West to the barbarians meant that *Romanitas* – what it meant to be a Roman – was being drained of meaning. Concessions to the fac-tionaries of the kind made by Anastasius only emphasized how feeble imperial control of the capital was. The centre was not holding. But, once Justinian was in power, he began to curb the activities of the circus factions, as a first step to restoring order on the streets of the capital.

THE REIGN OF JUSTINIAN I

Under Justinian clear lines of policy replaced the drift that had been characteristic of Anastasius's reign. His first significant action was to liquidate the schism that had cut off the church of Constantinople from the papacy. The restoration of ecclesiastical unity was a precondition for the restoration of political unity. Justinian may have hoped that the Germanic rulers of the West could be induced to abandon their Arian form of Christianity as a first step to their incorporation into the new Roman Empire. He developed personal ties with the Vandalic and Ostrogothic ruling families. This was self-defeating. It produced only a backlash, as the Germanic elite saw its privileged position under threat. Justinian turned to force. In 533 he dispatched his general Belisarius against the Vandalic kingdom of Carthage. The new Roman armies carried all before them. Carthage was captured in 534 and the Vandalic king was led back a captive to Constantinople, where he was paraded in triumph through the hippodrome. Belisarius then crossed over to Sicily and drove up through southern Italy to Rome. The Ostrogoths put up stiffer resistance than the Vandals, but in 540 Belisarius entered their capital of Ravenna in triumph. This was not the end of the story, for the Ostrogoths launched a counter-attack, which involved Italy in bitter warfare that lasted a dozen years and left the peninsula devastated. Justinian's armies fought through to eventual victory. Another army was able to secure the southern coasts of Spain. Despite enormous difficulties Justinian largely succeeded in bringing the western provinces – at least those around the Mediterranean – under his control. He had created a new Roman Empire – literally so, because it was ruled from the new Rome.

Justinian had no intention of restoring a Western Empire with its capital in Rome or Ravenna. He may have presented his policies in terms of a restoration, or *renovatio*, of the Roman Empire, but this conforms to that rule of thumb that suggests that the most radical measures are taken by those claiming to restore the past. Justinian's sense of being a Roman was the product of a new Rome, which may superficially and schematically have been modelled on the old, but which was entirely different in character. It was shaped by a Christian ideology of kingship, not by any nostalgia for the Augustan settlement. Justinian's building projects make this clear. They were directed, in the first instance, towards turning Constantinople into a fittingly Christian capital to match the new dispensation. The city that he inherited still bore the impress of the emperors of the Theodosian dynasty. Their monuments – columns that displayed their deeds in relief, triumphal archways, forums – were all Roman in inspiration. Even their churches conformed to the type of the Roman basilica.

When Justinian came to power there was hardly a dome in sight. By his death in 565 Constantinople's skyline was dominated by domed buildings, the most magnificent of which was the Church of St Sophia. He was given his opportunity to set his stamp on Constantinople by the Nika Riots of 532, which had resulted in the destruction of the heart of the capital between the forum of Constantine and the Augustaion. The old Cathedral of St Sophia and the whole area north of it, including the Church of St Eirene, were burnt down. These riots were sparked off by the circus factions, who objected to the measures taken by Justinian to discipline their activities. The Emperor's opponents from the senatorial aristocracy used the factions' dissatisfaction as a cover for their political ambitions. They had one of Anastasius's nephews proclaimed emperor. Justinian had been inclined to placate the factionaries, but now, prompted by his empress, Theodora, he set about ruthless repression. He sent his guards, under the command of Belisarius, into the hippodrome, where they are said to have massacred 30,000 people. He had his most prominent political opponents executed and confiscated the property of other senators. As a result of the Nika Riots, Justinian had not only complete control of his capital, but also a wonderful opportunity for building.

He had the entire area in and around the Augustaion rebuilt. This was the ceremonial heart of the city. Almost down to the final fall of the city its shape and appearance remained that stamped upon it by Justinian. His memory is still preserved in the shape of the great Church of St Sophia. Work began almost as soon as the Nika Riots were over and building was completed in just five years, which is an amazingly short period of time, given the church's size and complexity. Contemporaries were impressed not only by the scale of the building and by the lavishness of its decoration, but also by the novelty of its planning. This was the work of two mathematicians, Anthemius of Tralles and Isidore of Miletus. The church was a domed basilica, but so arranged around the central core as to leave the onlooker with the impression of a building not aligned on a particular axis but unified beneath the colossal dome. The historian Procopius's description of the church, which has never been bettered, states that the dome seemed 'somehow to hover in the air on no firm basis'.

The main body of the nave beneath the dome provided a fitting stage for the meeting of the emperor and his court, and the patriarch and his clergy, on the great festivals of the Christian year. The mingling of imperial and Christian liturgy beneath the dome of St Sophia was the more impressive for the light that played upon the participants. It streamed in through the ring of windows set in the rim of the dome and through the tiers of windows in the clerestories, and bounced off the gold mosaic of the dome and the marble cladding of the walls. Again according to Procopius, the effect was 'not that it was illuminated from outside by the sun, rather that the radiance was created from within itself'.

In the course of the celebration of the mass, patriarch and emperor would meet just outside the sanctuary and exchange the 'Kiss of Peace'. This symbolized the harmony that Justinian insisted must exist between the emperor and the church if the empire was to fulfil its role in the divine unfolding of history. It was a concept of church–state relations that Justinian elaborated in the preamble to his *Novel VI*. It begins: 'Among the greatest gifts of God bestowed by the kindness of Heaven are the priesthood and the imperial dignity. Of these, the former serves things divine; the latter rules human affairs and cares for them.' Justinian insisted that church and empire formed a harmonious unity by virtue of a clearly delineated division of labour. This may have contained a largish element of wishful thinking, but it had the effect of irrevocably fusing church and state.

Justinian's greatest achievement was his codification of Roman law. This again was carried out with amazing speed, thanks to the abilities of the panel of lawyers Justinian assembled, with Tribonian at the head. The first codification was ready in 529 and a second by 534. These were complemented by the *Digest* and *Institutes*, completed in 533. The former was a handbook of jurisprudence and the latter a legal textbook. Although presented as a return to the roots of classical Roman law, Justinian's work reshaped the law so that it could support a Christian monarchy. He himself drafted most of the legislation relating to the church and religion. Roman law lost much of its independence. If Justinian continued to subscribe to the notion that the emperor as an individual was bound by the law, he insisted that the emperor by virtue of his office was the law incarnate. The law was bridled by the absolutist ideology of Christian monarchy, and given concrete form by the equestrian statue that Justinian had erected of himself outside the Church of St Sophia: in his left hand he held an orb surmounted by a cross, the symbol of his universal authority and its divine origin.

During the opening period of his reign, with the help of the wonderfully talented team of experts he collected around him,

Justinian carried everything before him. His armies entered Carthage, Rome and Ravenna in triumph; the reunification of the empire seemed to be at hand. He organized theological conferences that appeared to offer solutions to the doctrinal divisions within the church. He articulated an ideology of empire, which embraced both law and theology, and constructed a fitting stage for its enactment. He created the ideal of the Christian Roman Empire, which would remain the foundation and inspiration of Byzantium. Perhaps he overreached himself. At the dedication of St Sophia in December 537 he is supposed to have murmured, 'Solomon, I have surpassed you.'

If this was so, then these words contained a deal of hubris. Circumstances turned against him. In 541 the Ostrogoths revolted in Italy. It took Justinian's generals some dozen years to master the situation. Italy suffered terrible devastation and Rome lost much of its former magnificence as it passed from one side to the other. The struggle was so protracted because Justinian was faced with a renewal of the war along the eastern frontier with the Sassanian dynasty of Iran, while the Danube frontier threatened to give way under pressure from the Slav tribes. These were a people making their first appearance on the stage of history as they started to pour out from their original homeland in and around the Pripet marshes. But the main danger was more insidious. In 541 bubonic plague struck Egypt and the next year spread through the eastern provinces and reached Constantinople, where it took a terrible toll. Procopius lived through it and reckoned that at its height 5,000 people a day were dying. It paralyzed government and society for at least three years. Justinian himself fell ill, but recovered and devised ingenious expedients to meet the disruption the plague produced. However, having overcome the immediate difficulties it presented, he had to face a bitter personal tragedy. In June 548 his consort, Empress Theodora, died. It took him several years to get over the loss.

Justinian's last years were grim. The bubonic plague recurred at irregular intervals. It sapped the economic and demographic foundations of the empire and undermined the viability of the *polis*, which had been at the heart of provincial life. As important as its social and economic effects was the psychological impact. From Procopius's detailed account of the plague at Constantinople we learn that the doctors despaired of their science. There was nothing they could do to combat the disease. People crowded into the churches as the best hope of protection. Despite fleeing to safer areas at its approach, another historian of the time lost most of his family in outbreaks of the plague; its unpredictability left him with only God to turn to. There was a feeling that God was punishing his people for their sins. Justinian reissued legislation against homosexuality, which prescribed the death penalty. He felt that his empire might suffer the same fate as the cities of the plain – Sodom and Gomorrah – and for the same reason.

Justinian had always been intensely pious. He drank little but water; he ate sparingly – only vegetables, pickles, and herbs, according to one account – and did with a minimum of sleep. He delighted in the company of monks, and theology provided him with his favourite topic of conversation. He once suffered from an infected knee brought on by strenuous devotions during Lent. On another occasion – it may have been when he fell ill with the plague – the doctors despaired of his life. But the doctor saints, Cosmas and Damian, appeared to him in a vision and he recovered. He had their shrine outside Constantinople rebuilt and made a pilgrimage to it. In 563, he made another pilgrimage to the shrine of the Archangel Michael at Germe, deep in Anatolia. He was eighty at the time. It was an extraordinary thing to do for somebody who since his teens had hardly ever travelled outside the environs of the capital.

Justinian's strength of character is evident from the way in which he faced up to the crises of the middle part of his reign and very largely overcame them. Symbolic of this was his reaction to the collapse of the dome of St Sophia in 558: he had it rebuilt, and the church was rededicated four years later. The achievements of the early part of his reign were tested, but shown to be basically sound. The effort to preserve them only drew out more clearly their true meaning and their radical character. The emphasis was on Christianity. Justinian devoted an enormous amount of his time to problems of theology in the hope of bringing peace to the church. He went a very long way towards mollifying the Monophysites by condemning orthodox theologians who appeared to overemphasize the humanity of Christ. This was not to the liking of the papacy. When in 553 Justinian convened a new General Council at Constantinople, he coerced the pope of the day into accepting the formula that Christ might be perfect man and perfect God, 'distinct but inseparable', but at the deepest level of being he was one. Under Justinian's guidance Constantinople was evolving its own distinctive theology, which over the next three centuries would be more creative than that of Alexandria or Rome.

Justinian accomplished almost as much as any living man can, but towards the end of his life seemed to have nothing new to offer. He was isolated and unpopular – the fate of rulers, however great, who have lived too long – and his death in 565 was a relief. He was succeeded by his nephew Justin, who tried to distance himself from his uncle's unpopularity. However, Justin's attempt to reverse the passive foreign policy of Justinian's last years was ill judged. It led to a breakdown in relations with the Sassanian Empire, a weakening of the Danube frontier and, ultimately, the Lombard invasion of Italy, which undid much of Justinian's work. Justin's failures contributed to his mental collapse and his replacement by Tiberius, a member of his staff. Tiberius reigned briefly (578–82) and was succeeded by his son-in-law, Maurice (582–602), who happened to be one of the few successful generals of the age. These emperors in their different ways struggled to preserve Justinian's legacy. Though more protracted, it was a period not unlike the middle years of Justinian's reign, when the struggle to overcome all kinds of difficulties was

27

fuelled by the necessity to preserve, as a religious obligation, the Christian empire and its capital, the new Rome. In this there was complete continuity with Justinian's reign. None of these emperors had the opportunity to build on the scale of Justinian in the early part of his reign, but they continued in the same tradition of patronizing saints' shrines and emphasizing the emperor's closeness to Christ. Justin II added a new throne room to the Chrysotriklinos, the main reception hall of the Great Palace. The throne stood in an apse under a mosaic of Christ and emphasized the emperor's role as Christ's deputy on earth. This was very much in line with the conception of the imperial office that was elaborated by Justinian. It was complemented by the way that the symbols of the imperial office were losing their Roman imprint. Emperor Maurice substituted the image of the Mother of God for a Roman victory on the imperial seal. He may also have been responsible for setting up an image of Christ over the Chalke Gate, the main ceremonial entrance into the imperial palace.

ICONS

There was a distinct enthusiasm at the imperial court for Christian images, or icons. Justin II had a famous icon of Christ, which had been kept in the Cappadocian town of Kamoulianai, brought to Constantinople in 574. It was popularly believed to be a miraculous image of the kind known as *acheiropoietos* (unmanufactured), which were supposed to have been created by divine agency. The most famous was the Mandylion of Edessa, which was a cloth bearing the imprint of Christ's face. Legend had it that the ruler of Edessa had asked Christ for his portrait. He duly obliged by miraculously leaving his features on a napkin he used to wipe his face. The Kamoulianai image would in due course be used as a battle standard in the wars against the Sassanians.

The adoption of icons as symbols of state at the end of the sixth century was another sign of the transformation of the Roman Empire into a Christian empire, but it was also a sign of the consequent transformation of Christianity. The early church was very suspicious of religious imagery. Christians made do with a rather limited repertoire borrowed from Jews and pagans alike. It was only after Constantine's conversion that a Christian art started to come into its own, but there remained intense suspicion of art for personal use because it approached too close to idolatry. Constantine's sister consulted Eusebius of Caesarea about obtaining an image of Christ for private devotion. The churchman reproved her, because now that Christ reigned in glory he should only be contemplated in the mind. Even public decoration of churches earned reproof from Epiphanius of Salamis (d. 403), one of the most respected fathers of the church. He feared that a popular taste for images was a way in which pagan practices and manner of thinking could infiltrate Christian worship.

Others were, however, coming to accept that church decoration served a useful purpose as the 'books of the illiterate'. Their value was also apparent with the growth of various saints' cults in the aftermath of Constantine's conversion. These may have centred on the relics of the saint, but they required visualization of the saint in the full flower of life. In a sermon on St Theodore the Recruit, Gregory of Nyssa (d. c. 395) imagined the reaction of those who glimpsed the saint's relics: 'They embraced them as though they were the living body itself in its full flower; they brought eye, mouth, ear, all their senses into play. Then shedding tears of reverence and passion, they addressed to the martyr their prayer of intercession, as if he were hale and present.' Gregory noted that around the tomb were images of the saint. The image seemed a natural adjunct of the relic and the saint's cult. Images might be given greater validity by having a little of the dust from relics worked into the paint. Just as cures were often effected by drinking a draught of water mixed with dust from relics, so we read in the Miracles of St Cosmas and Damian of a woman who scraped some of the paint off a depiction of the saints, mixed it with water, drank it and was cured of her ailment.

In practice, there were initially some hesitations about the role of images in the cult of a saint, as we can see from the Life of St Daniel the Stylite. Daniel was a Syrian holy man who came to play an influential role in the religious and political life of mid-fifth-century Constantinople. He angrily rejected an attempt by one of his admirers to set up his image over a private chapel and to write an account of his life while he was still alive. But the saint was happy to accept a silver icon of himself weighing 10 pounds as a thanks-offering from a family he had healed. The difference seems to be that on the first occasion the saint felt that the admirer was trying to take over his sanctity, whereas on the second occasion the image was placed in a church that was central to his cult. These episodes reveal that by the mid-fifth century the image had a part – perhaps a slightly contentious one – to play in the promotion of saints' cults.

All the evidence suggests that the figurative decoration of churches and the appearance of individual portraits of Christ, his mother, and his saints were natural and spontaneous developments, which became an accepted part of Christian worship from the late fourth century onwards. But even in the early sixth century there remained doubts among the ecclesiastical hierarchy as to the validity of this practice. There was disquiet at the way people were putting up paintings and carvings in the sanctuaries of churches and thus 'once again disturbing divine tradition'. It was, however, agreed that they served the useful purpose of instructing the illiterate. The educated, on the other hand, would derive more from 'holy writings', which were seen as possessing superior spiritual value.

The evidence also suggests that Justinian's long reign was a turning point in official attitudes towards religious art. In the early years there was still suspicion of figurative art; by the end of his reign it was coming to infiltrate all aspects of Christian worship. Official approval now extended to icons: individual pictures of Christ, his mother, and his saints. These might form part of a larger church decoration but they might also be the focus of private devotions, even if displayed in a public place, as was the case with certain special images kept in churches or monasteries. It was the icon, rather than the whole sweep of Christian art, that raised the question of the legitimacy of art in Christian worship, because the dangers of devotion spilling over into idolatry were most evident with icons.

Hardly any early icons survive, with the exception of a few connected with Sinai and Rome. These normally used the encaustic technique (pigments suspended in wax), which was favoured in classical painting and disappeared from the eighth century. We can therefore be fairly confident that icons on which it is employed date back to the sixth and seventh centuries. They are often very fine and continue the highest traditions of classical portraiture, but we have to turn to the written sources to discover their purpose and their aura.

It is hardly a coincidence that from the late sixth century a variety of sources commented on icons as though they were an accepted part of Christian piety and worship, whereas earlier there were only sporadic references. It is no surprise either that hagiography of one form or another provides the greater part of the information, given the close connections that existed between icons and the cult of saints.

The most informative piece of hagiography for our purposes is the Life of St Theodore of Sykeon. Theodore was born in Galatia early in Justinian's reign and died in 613. His Life was written shortly afterwards by one of his followers. It was designed to preserve his memory and promote his cult. It was not a history, but, as happens with hagiography, it contains much in the way of incidental detail. There is no particular stress on images; there is much more on the saint's asceticism, on his role as a holy man and a healer, on visions, on processions and pilgrimages, on the importance of the Eucharist. There are only half a dozen episodes involving images in the whole text, but they are instructive and reveal that icons had become the natural accompaniment to many aspects of Christian worship. Aged twelve, Theodore was a victim of the plague. His family despaired of his life and dragged him into a local church, where they laid him at the entrance to the sanctuary. Above him there happened to be an image of Christ, from which drops of moisture fell on him and effected a miraculous cure. A few years later Theodore was having the greatest difficulty in memorizing the Psalter. Not even the tranquillity of a chapel was any help. He threw himself on the ground in front of an image of Christ and sought his aid. All at once he felt a sweetness in his mouth, which he recognized as the grace of God. He swallowed it as though partaking of the Eucharist. He had no more trouble in learning the Psalter.

Icons were associated with other religious phenomena, such as visions. So, Theodore was lying ill in bed. On the wall above his bed was an icon of the doctor saints, Cosmas and Damian. Theodore became delirious and saw the saints walking out of their icons. They examined him in the way that a doctor might. He begged them to intercede on his behalf with the king, who was, of course, Christ himself. Their intervention worked and Theodore was healed. By the turn of the sixth century images were also part of the paraphernalia of pilgrimage at various shrines. Theodore went on pilgrimage to the Pisidian town of Sozopolis. Its main attraction was a wonder-working icon of the Mother of God, which sprayed out myrrh. Theodore stood in front of the icon and his eyes and face were showered with myrrh. The onlookers took this as a sign that he truly was a worthy servant of God.

This was one way in which an icon could confirm sanctity. Another was to have an icon of the saint painted, as somebody healed by Theodore did in gratitude. More revealing is an incident that occurred when Theodore was staying in a monastery in Constantinople. He already had a far-flung reputation as a miracle worker. The monks wanted a memorial of the great man's stay with them, so they hired an artist, who sketched the saint through the keyhole of his cell. When Theodore was departing, the abbot asked him to bless the icon that had been produced. The saint smiled and said, 'You are a great thief, for what are you doing except stealing something?' Theodore believed that the icon had stolen something of his virtue, but he was flattered rather than offended. He gave his blessing and went his way. The meaning of this incident is made even clearer by an episode from another contemporary Life, that of St Symeon the Stylite the Younger, who died in 592. One of his devotees set up an icon of the saint in her house, where 'it worked miracles, being shadowed over by the holy spirit that dwelt in the saint'.

Other episodes from the Life of St Theodore of Sykeon are paralleled in another contemporary hagiography, the Miracles of St Demetrius. The cult of Demetrius, the patron saint of Thessaloniki, centred on a cenotaph in the crypt of his church. An image of the saint had to do service for his relics, which notoriously had never been found. His Miracles contain stories in which men have seen the saint riding to the rescue of his city, looking just as he did in his icons by way of authentification. In another vision he was described as 'wearing a toga and displaying a rosy gracious countenance, distributing his favours to the people like some consul to whom the Emperor has delegated plenary powers'. This is exactly how he appears in one of the surviving panels that decorated the nave of his church. There are also icons of the saint on the pillars of the nave as you approach the sanctuary. They show the saint with his votaries; one may be Archbishop John, who, at the turn of the sixth century, was responsible for compiling the first cycle of the saint's miracles. The surviving mosaics from the Church of St Demetrius at Thessaloniki are proof of the place that the image had in the development of the cult of a local saint.

The image was, however, not only central to the cult of saints; it also seemed to unify all facets of Christian worship in Byzantium.

It could be used to communicate the meaning of the faith in its different aspects. The essential role that images had come to assume was emphasized by the way some images acquired miraculous powers. This was an extraordinary development, but quite logical once it was accepted that the image provided a means of communication with the world of the spirit. Communication is a two-way process, so it was fair to assume that in some cases images might be a channel for the action of divine grace in this world. This was taken to its logical conclusion with the assumption that something of a saint's special power might inhere in his or her image.

It would be difficult to separate such an outlook from pagan assumptions about the role of cult objects. It has therefore been normal to see the rise of the cult of images in sixth-century Byzantium as part of the re-emergence of older patterns of thought and to have been largely popular in origin. There is bound to be some truth to this. However, it is clear that by the mid-sixth century the promotion of images was the work of the elite. The historian Agathias has left an epigram on an icon of the Archangel Michael. It was probably a thanks-offering made as he was taking his final exams in the 550s. Its interest lies in part in the way it justifies the place that icons were assuming in private devotions. Agathias claimed that 'art is able through colours to act as a ferry for the prayer of the heart'. He accepted that it was a link in the process of intercession by 'directing the mind to a higher state of imagination'. In a few elegant phrases Agathias sets out the so-called 'anagogic' justification for images: the idea that art can act as a means of access to higher things.

The corollary of this was that reverence did not go to the image itself but to the reality behind the image. Agathias expresses the excitement felt by a young intellectual of Justinian's day about the possibility of the icon opening up a pathway of communication that had once been the preserve of the mystic and the ascetic. Agathias had little difficulty in combining an enthusiasm for the latest forms of Christian piety with showing off traditional literary skills. In this way Justinian's reign was a point of balance. Classical culture continued, but the experimentation that went on in so many fields would soon reveal how irrelevant it was becoming. The themes of classical art were reduced to kitsch and its thought to an extended topos.

Nowhere was this clearer than in imperial art. The old imperial imagery continued, but seemed increasingly out of date because it failed to integrate imperial authority into a specifically Christian dispensation. Justinian responded by elaborating new themes of imperial art. He built on the devotion to the cult of saints that had been a feature of the imperial family from the fifth century. Emperor Leo I honoured the Mother of God by adding a reliquary chapel to her Church of the Blachernai to house her veil. Above the precious relic he placed an image of Mary showing the emperor and his family in attendance. This was at a time when there was still opposition to the use of images from some sections of the ecclesiastical hierarchy. But this was less important than the need felt by an emperor to associate himself with a new source of power, in this case the cult of the Mother of God. An image was the most obvious way of proclaiming his allegiance. The first tentative steps to create a more relevant imperial imagery were thus being taken in the mid-fifth century.

The example of Leo I suggests that by associating himself with his family he was acting in a personal capacity rather than presenting the full face of Roman imperial authority. But this is exactly what Justinian and Theodora show in the famous panels in the sanctuary of the Church of San Vitale at Ravenna. On one side there is a representation of Justinian and his court; on the other, Theodora and hers. They are both shown in procession. Justinian is surrounded by clerics, one of whom is identified as Maximian, Archbishop of Ravenna, and, bringing up the rear, members of the imperial bodyguard. The Emperor clasps a paten in his hand. Theodora is attended by her ladies-in-waiting and holds a chalice. The skirt of her cloak is embroidered with figures of the Magi. She stands under a canopy and to her right a male attendant pushes aside a curtain to reveal a courtyard with a fountain. These scenes are best interpreted as an idealized version of the ceremony of the Great Entrance, when an emperor and empress enter the Church of St Sophia bearing gifts, like the Magi. The meaning of the panels was that Justinian and Theodora also participated mystically in the liturgy of the Church of San Vitale. Impressive as they are as a statement of Christian majesty, the 'imperial court' does not seem to have entered the repertoire of imperial art at Byzantium. There were local circumstances that explain the presence of the panels in the Church of San Vitale. The church was designed as a statement of orthodoxy directed against the Arian occupation of Ravenna by the Ostrogoths. The main Arian church (now called San Apollinare Nuovo) originally showed along the walls of the nave processions headed by the Ostrogothic king Theodorich and by his queen. The Justinian and Theodora panels were designed to counter this. Work on the Church of San Vitale may have been begun in the 520s, when Ravenna was still the Ostrogothic capital. It was not consecrated until 547. By that time Ravenna had returned to Byzantine rule. The panels therefore took on an additional significance: they proclaimed that orthodox rule had been restored.

It is possible to dismiss the Justinian and Theodora panels as experimentation, but they pointed to the way that new meaning was being given to the imperial image and the imperial office by associating them unequivocally with Christ, who presides in majesty over the Church of San Vitale from the apse. Imperial authority was a reflection of the divine, just as the earthly order was a reflection of the heavenly. Paradoxically, both art and literature portray heaven as a reflection of the imperial palace.

The notion of this world somehow being a dim and distant reflection of the perfections of the heavenly world was best caught through works of art, which served as transmitters for the prayers of the faithful and for the answering signals sent down from on high. The triumph of the icon in the sixth century was interwoven with the crystallization of a Byzantine civilization. It was far from being a victory of superstition or pagan revanchism. It provided the best means of expressing the essentials of a new order and a new outlook. It centred on an imperial authority that was divinely inspired, on an imperial capital that was divinely protected, and on a church where heaven and earth mingled. It was marked by a profound sense of order and hierarchy, which was best conveyed through ritual and art. This was the essence of Justinian's achievement.

Chapter Three

THE PARTING OF THE WAYS

The history of the Mediterranean world is one of unity and diversity. For a time Rome had been able to unite the Mediterranean world, but by the third century the city was no longer fulfilling this role. In the fifth and sixth centuries Constantinople took its place, although its dominance was never as assured as Rome's had been. The political authority of the emperor at Constantinople scarcely touched the barbarian kingdoms that arose in the West in the course of the fifth century. Culturally, the Mediterranean would seem more diverse in the sixth century than it had in the Age of the Antonines, when Rome was at the height of its power. This was largely a function of Christianity, which transformed classical culture, giving it a new direction and quality. Christianity not only favoured Greek at the expense of Latin, but also created Syriac and Coptic cultures in Syria and Egypt respectively. It is easy to discern the fault lines, which would widen in the course of the seventh and eighth centuries to create the separate civilizations characteristic of the medieval world. In this process Justinian had a role to play, because he asserted the unity of the Mediterranean world for the last time, in this instance under the aegis of the emperor of Constantinople and Christianity. His work provided a cultural unity from which the different medieval civilizations derived much of their cultural capital. However reluctantly, the elites of all regions round the Mediterranean continued to look to Constantinople as the centre of their world. Though the cultural dominance of Byzantium waned from the end of the sixth century, it remained a factor into the ninth century, by which time the Carolingian West and the Abbasid caliphate sought to emulate and surpass Byzantium rather than imitate it.

THE COLLAPSE OF CITY LIFE

Byzantium managed to survive setbacks that threatened to overwhelm it. It was a rearguard action that ensured the continuing respect of surrounding powers, but the beginnings of its decline can be traced back to the aftermath of Justinian's reign. Thereafter, with brief exceptions, Byzantium was under pressure. Justinian's death in 565 coincided with the appearance of a new force along the Danube frontier. This came in the shape of the Avars, another central Asian people, who were able to fill the vacuum left by the break-up of the Hunnic confederation more than a century earlier. They brought the local Slav tribes under their control, while shunting the Lombards, hitherto loyal allies of Byzantium, westwards towards Italy. In 568 the Lombards occupied the Po Valley, which became known as Lombardy. They then pushed south, confining Byzantine authority to the areas around Ravenna, Rome and Bari. Much of the territory won at such a cost by Justinian's armies was lost at a stroke. This did not mean that the imperial government at Constantinople was inclined to abandon Justinian's achievements. Far from it: the western territories were organized under military governors known as exarchs, who exercised viceregal powers from their capitals of Ravenna and Carthage. These exarchates help to explain why Byzantium maintained a foothold in the West for so long.

At the same time the war against the Sassanians in the East flared up. Conflict between Constantinople and Ctesiphon was inevitable, given the difficulties of dividing the Fertile Crescent between the two powers. This was a struggle that had been going on from at least the fifth century BC. In many ways the struggle between the Sassanians and Byzantium was a dress rehearsal for the wars between Islam and Byzantium.

Justinian's successors had to respond not only to external pressures but also to deep internal divisions, which showed themselves most obviously in the shape of religious disputes. The peace that Justinian imposed upon the church was deceptive. The Monophysites of Syria and Egypt exploited it to create their own ecclesiastical organization. The revival of the war with the Sassanians cast doubt – quite unnecessarily – on their loyalties. The authorities in Constantinople were disturbed by the way that the Monophysite church was coming under the patronage of the Ghassanids, an Arab tribe from the Yemen that established itself along Syria's desert frontier in the early sixth century. The Ghassanids had been picked out by Justinian for special favour and their chieftain was given the title of phylarch. They were responsible for the defence of the desert frontier but their Monophysite sympathies made them increasingly suspect. Finally, in 584 Emperor Maurice moved against them and dissolved the Ghassanid phylarchy. This not only alienated the Monophysite church, but also threatened the stability of the eastern frontier, with, as we shall see, fateful consequences.

There were other signs of dissatisfaction. There were a series of army mutinies and growing urban unrest, which took the form of factional rivalries and was not limited to the capital but spread throughout the empire. Circus factions began to appear in any good-sized city. They do not seem to have had any clear social or religious affiliations, but they provided an outlet for youthful violence, which could at the same time be used by local leaders. At Constantinople, and perhaps elsewhere, they came to constitute a militia, which gave them greater power.

This volatile mixture ignited at the start of the seventh century.

Emperor Maurice ordered his army to winter beyond the Danube. The intention was to bring the Slav tribes of the area to heel. The armies mutinied and marched on Constantinople under the leadership of a centurion called Phokas. Within the city Maurice was confronted by an uprising of the circus factions, who brought Phokas to power. Maurice and members of his family were put to death. This was the signal for factional rivalry to erupt into gang warfare. The slogans of the factions were incised on the walls of public buildings, churches and theatres; examples of this graffiti survive from cities along the western seaboard of Asia Minor, and from Crete, Syria, Palestine and Egypt. A variety of formulae was used; 'Victory to the Fortune of the Greens' and 'May the Lord help Phokas, our God-crowned emperor, and the Blues' are typical. In one instance the word 'Blues' has been scratched out and replaced by 'Greens'.

This empire-wide outburst of urban violence brings us face to face with the death throes of the *polis*, which had remained at the centre of provincial life and administration until the late sixth century. Its demise was another side to the transformation of the Mediterranean world, which was clearly marked in the case of Byzantium. The Eastern Empire can be envisaged as a network of cities around its hub, Constantinople. Cities had changed, in the sense that the old municipal institutions had disappeared, and in the sense that there had also been some degree of rationalization. Those cities that had no role to play in the imperial administration suffered, since their functioning depended to a considerable extent on imperial largesse. City organization depended increasingly on the bishop working in conjunction with an imperial governor and a few local notables. In most cases the urban fabric of the great cities of antiquity was maintained to the end of the sixth century. Archaeology provides evidence of ordinary dwellings being refurbished at exactly this moment at both Corinth and Ephesus.

This was a façade, as became clear with the rapid collapse of city life in the first half of the seventh century. The apparent cause was often foreign invasion. In the Peloponnese, in the face of Avar and Slav attacks, the inhabitants of Sparta, under their bishop, retreated at the end of the sixth century to the safety of Monemvasia, a virtually impregnable rock with communications to the capital by sea. In Asia Minor the Persian invasions meant the withdrawal to a defensible acropolis. Cities turned into *kastra*, or fortresses, which normally sheltered the bishop and his cathedral. A good example is the ancient city of Didyma, known to the Byzantines as Hieron: it turned into a fortified church, a small castle, and a hamlet. This marked a decisive shift in the balance between city and countryside in favour of the latter. *Kastra* progressively replaced the *polis*, its weaknesses exposed by the lack of security. This transformation was more or less completed by the middle of the seventh century, when city life had either retreated to the core of the empire around the Sea of Marmora or survived in a few outposts, such as Thessaloniki, Ephesus, and Ravenna, but on a much reduced scale. At Ephesus the new walls enclosed an area less than half the size of the ancient city, and the huge cathedral was replaced by a new church only half its size, in keeping with the reduced size of the city. The network of cities around Constantinople was radically simplified. Most urban functions were now concentrated in the capital, which made it more dominant than ever and marked the character of Byzantine culture and society. The broadly based urban culture of late antiquity gave way to a narrow metropolitan one. It was both Byzantium's strength and weakness. Decisive for these developments was the reign of the emperor Heraclius (610–41).

HERACLIUS AND THE SASSANIANS

Heraclius came from the eastern frontiers of the Byzantine Empire, but his father had been appointed exarch of Carthage. It was from there that Heraclius set out to rescue the empire from Phokas. In

610 he entered Constantinople in triumph, thanks to the support of the patriarch Sergius and the Green faction, which had fallen out with Phokas. The difficulties confronting Heraclius were enormous: the Avars were rampaging through the Balkans and their Slav tributaries were settling in numbers; the Sassanians occupied much of Anatolia. The chronicler Theophanes tells us that Heraclius was at a loss to know what to do. The army had been reduced to two detachments. He could not drive back the Sassanians, who went from strength to strength. In 613 Damascus fell to them; the next year it was Jerusalem's turn, and in 619 Egypt was conquered. The eastern provinces fell with worrying ease. The position seemed untenable. In 618 Heraclius threatened to abandon Constantinople and return to Carthage.

By now, however, the war against the Sassanians was being treated as a war of religion. Byzantine propaganda had the Sassanian King of Kings Chosroes II turning down Heraclius's overtures for peace with these contemptuous words: 'I will have no mercy upon you until you renounce him who was crucified and worship the sun.' Heraclius was persuaded to stay by Patriarch Sergius and the people of the city. It was a demonstration of the solidarity of patriarch and people, and an appeal to a common loyalty to the Mother of God, the protector of Constantinople. Heraclius was reminded that emperors had a special responsibility for the promotion of her cult. Her two most precious relics – her veil and her girdle – had been brought from the Holy Land under imperial auspices and entrusted to the safekeeping of the churches of the Blachernai and the Chalkoprateiai respectively. These churches had been repaired by Justin II, who seems to have done much to promote the cult of the Mother of God. Emperor Maurice later had established the Feast of the Dormition of the Virgin as one of the major celebrations of the Christian year. The concerted effort on the part of emperors in the late sixth century to promote the cult of the Mother of God at Constantinople was recognition that traditional imperial ceremonial associated with the hippodrome had to be balanced by specifically Christian ritual. Imperial participation in processions to the great shrines of the capital was the clearest acknowledgement of this need. It was also obvious that the imperial capital required the most powerful intercessor, who was, by common acknowledgement, the Mother of God. When Constantinople came under siege from the Avars and the Persians in 626, the people of the city turned to the Mother of God for protection. The Patriarch had her image painted on the gates of the city as an act of defiance. The enemy was driven off. Choirs intoned the Akathistos hymn in honour of the Mother of God, with a new opening specially composed by Patriarch Sergius crediting her with the victory, as its first lines make clear: 'I, your city, ascribe to you, Mother of God, the most mighty commander, the prize of victory and thanks for our deliverance from dire calamity.'

Heraclius began to display a greater confidence. In order to meet the Sassanian threat he embarked on a high-risk strategy. He left Constantinople in the care of the Patriarch and established his headquarters at Trebizond. He built up alliances with the Armenians and Georgians and an understanding with the Khazars, who were the dominant force on the steppe lands. With their help Heraclius was able to raid deep into Iraq towards the Sassanian capital of Ctesiphon. In 627 he won a great victory, which brought the Sassanians to their knees and forced them to sue for peace. Heraclius presented this as a victory for the cross over the fire-worshipping Sassanians. It was claimed that when they had conquered Jerusalem in 614 they had taken the relic of the true cross to Ctesiphon. The relic was now returned. Heraclius formally restored it to its rightful place in the Church of the Holy Sepulchre in a great ceremony in 631, the culmination of his victorious progress through the newly recovered eastern provinces. At the same time, in recognition that his imperial authority was Christian rather than Roman in origin, Heraclius took as his official title *basileus*.

The cornerstone of Heraclius's restoration in the aftermath of his victory over the Sassanians was his religious policy. Religion was always the most effective means of tying the provinces to the capital. However, during the years of Sassanian occupation the Monophysite church in Egypt and Syria had become increasingly powerful. It was unrealistic to expect them to accept Chalcedonian orthodoxy from Constantinople. Patriarch Sergius therefore developed a compromise formula: Christ might be perfect man and perfect God, but he possessed only a single energy. This was at first received with satisfaction by the Monophysites of Egypt. More surprisingly, it was also acceptable to the pope of the day. Of the patriarchates, only Jerusalem objected. Opposition became more vociferous once the new formula was enshrined in an imperial decree, the *Ecthesis* (638). It seemed as if the Emperor was usurping the function of a General Council of the Church, which alone had the authority to alter dogma. In any case, much had changed. In the early spring of 638 Jerusalem had fallen to a new power, Islam. When the patriarch Sophronius saw the Muslim leader Umur entering the city, he is supposed to have exclaimed, 'In truth, this is the abomination of the desolation established in the holy place, which Daniel the prophet spoke of.' This reflects the stunned reaction to the appearance of Islam. As early as 634 Heraclius had abandoned Syria in despair, transferring the Holy Cross from Jerusalem to Constantinople.

ISLAM

The rise of Islam is the most striking and important event of the Middle Ages. Initially, it could be explained only in apocalyptical terms. Its speed and completeness still staggers belief. The Arabs were well known to the Romans; their martial qualities were respected. For centuries before Islam they had been moving from the deserts of the Hejaz to the confines of the Fertile Crescent. The normal pattern was for the government at Constantinople to hire

Arab chieftains to guard the desert frontier. The Ghassanids had done this admirably until relations broke down with the imperial administration towards the end of the sixth century. This left Byzantium's eastern provinces vulnerable to attack, first to the Sassanians and then to the armies of Islam. Heraclius realized the importance of restoring his desert defences, but time was not on his side. A new wave of Arabs was about to burst out from the desert, but this time united under the battle cry, 'There is only one God, Allah, and Muhammad is his prophet.'

Muhammad's message provided the Arabs with a degree of unity that they had not previously possessed. It turned them into the new 'chosen people', with a mission to overturn the old dispensation represented by the Roman and Sassanian empires. The latter was even more vulnerable than the former. Its capital, Ctesiphon, was within striking distance of the desert. It fell in 637, following the Muslim victory at Qadisiyya. The Sassanians were in disarray. In 651 the Muslims hunted down and killed the last Sassanian king of kings, Yazdgird III. With that, the Islamic conquest of the Iranian plateau was effectively completed. The Byzantines lost Syria, Palestine, and Egypt just as swiftly. This was hardly surprising, given that at the beginning of the century Syria and Palestine had been in Persian hands for nearly twenty years, and Egypt for nearly ten. The restoration of Byzantine administration was still only at a preliminary stage when the armies of Islam struck. The loss of these provinces is often attributed to the disloyalty of the local Christian communities, which are supposed to have seen the Arabs as liberators from the Byzantine yoke. This is wide of the mark. These communities were simply following what had become traditional practice in the wars with the Persians: it was better to surrender and await the outcome of the war. The Byzantines had always returned victorious, but not this time. Instead, they found themselves pushed back into Anatolia by the forces of Islam. For a century they were involved in a life and death struggle to hold Anatolia against the Muslim armies. During this time Islam was able to evolve a glittering civilization, which not only made a full Byzantine recovery an impossibility, but also left Byzantium much diminished by comparison.

It probably made little difference that Heraclius's death in 641 was followed by a disputed succession at Constantinople. Islam's momentum was too powerful. Having secured the strongpoints of northern Syria, its armies pushed into Anatolia and Armenia. The Arabs took to the sea with the same elan as the Romans in their wars with the Carthaginians. They seized the island of Cyprus and in 655 defeated the Byzantine fleet at the Battle of the Masts off the south coast of Anatolia. It was a victory that would have opened up the eastern Mediterranean to Islam had it not been followed almost immediately by the assassination of the caliph, Uthman.

The ensuing civil war gave Byzantium temporary respite. Emperor Constans (641–68) was able to refortify some of the strategic points in Anatolia, but once Islam was reunited under Caliph Mu'awiya (661–80), the Muslim attacks began again. Constans despaired and did what his grandfather Heraclius had threatened to do: he abandoned Constantinople for the West in 662. The explanation at the time was that he wanted to transfer his capital to Rome. But after a state visit there, he made his headquarters in Sicily. The administration at Constantinople refused to allow Constans's sons to join him in Sicily, which meant that the empire was effectively divided. It is an intriguing episode, all the more important for the way Constans took the bulk of the Eastern army with him. It does seem that he had decided that Constantinople was untenable, but his move to the West earned him many enemies. He was murdered in his bath in 668.

It was left to his son Constantine IV (668–85) at Constantinople to face a concerted effort on the part of Caliph Mu'awiya to conquer the city. The Muslim navy secured the sea lanes linking the ports of Syria to the Sea of Marmora, where in 670 it was able to establish an advanced base at Kyzikos. For seven years Constantinople was under blockade, but the final assault in 678 failed, thanks to the effectiveness of 'liquid' or 'Greek fire', which seems to have been very like napalm. Combustible materials made of petroleum had long been used in the Near East. What was new was the means of propulsion. Pumps were now used to propel a combustible mixture, which ignited under pressure, through a tube. The mechanism seems not unlike that of a soda siphon, and was the invention of a refugee from Syria called Kallinikos. Its effects were devastating. It saved Constantinople and gave Byzantium a decisive advantage in defence. It was one of the empire's state secrets. The Muslim armies were thoroughly mauled as they retreated from Constantinople across Anatolia, while their fleet was caught in a storm and went to the bottom off the treacherous coasts of south-western Asia Minor. It was a comprehensive defeat for Islam, which restored Byzantine prestige. The rulers of the West, from the Khagan of the Avars downwards, sent envoys to Constantinople seeking peace. For the time being the initiative passed once again to Byzantium. Caliph Mu'awiya found himself with a rebellion on his hands, which threatened his capital city of Damascus. This was the work of a mysterious Christian group known as the Mardaites, who had established themselves in the mountains of Lebanon.

A FRAGILE PEACE

The victory of 678 gave Constantine IV the opportunity to reorganize his empire. Most important was the need to restore ecclesiastical unity. The alienation of the church in the West from Constantinople, just as much as Constans II's decision to move his capital to the West, emphasized the fragmentation of the empire in the face of the Muslim advance.

Although Heraclius's religious policy initially had the support of the papacy, by the time his grandson Constans II revived it in his decree known as the *Typos* (648) Rome had become the major centre of opposition. The papacy now objected to the formula – the Monothelete formula, as it has come to be known – that had Christ united by a single will and energy. Rome was taking on the mantle of Jerusalem, which had been the original source of criticism. This was partly because in the aftermath of the fall of Jerusalem to the Muslims, many Palestinian clergy found refuge in Italy, attracted in part by Pope Theodore I (642–9), who was of Palestinian origin. At the centre of opposition was a Palestinian monk, Maximos the Confessor, one of the great Byzantine theologians. Born in the late sixth century, Maximos's early training was in the monasteries of Palestine, but at some point he made his way to Constantinople and entered imperial service. It was not unknown for monks to be included in the imperial entourage. However, the attractions of monastic life proved too strong for Maximos and by 618 he had retired to a monastery near the capital. These were years of Sassanian invasions. In 626 Maximos fled from Asia Minor to the safety of North Africa. His reputation as a theologian grew and was enhanced by a public debate that took place in 645 at Carthage. He convinced the exarch, who was presiding, that he should oppose the Monothelete line imposed from Constantinople. Maximos was also behind the Lateran Council of 649 convened by Pope Martin I (649–53), and he drew up the acts of this council, which condemned Constans II's *Typos*.

Constans reacted by ordering the Exarch of Ravenna to arrest Maximos and Pope Martin. The exarch refused and continued in his defiance until his death in 652. A new exarch was sent out, who did carry out imperial orders. Martin was dispatched to Constantinople, where he was condemned for treason and exiled to the Crimea. Maximos, who resolutely refused to recognize imperial authority in matters of dogma, was dealt with in similar fashion. He eventually died in 662 in some remote place of exile in the Caucasus. Constans's ruthless treatment of Martin and Maximos brought Rome to heel, but produced lasting resentment.

When Constantine IV called a General Council of the Church in the aftermath of his victory over Islam in 678, his aim was reconciliation: reconciliation within the church, and reconciliation with the papacy and the patriarch of Jerusalem, which had been the main centres of opposition to the Monothelete policy. The council duly convened at the end of 680. Monotheletism was condemned, in accordance with a tome issued by Pope Agathon. The ideal of ecclesiastical unity was restored. How brittle it was soon became clear during the first reign of Constantine IV's son, Justinian II (685–95).

For all his father's achievements – victory over the forces of Islam and bringing peace to the church – Justinian II is engraved far more vividly on the historical record and not just for his trade mark of a golden nose. He hoped to capitalize on his father's success to complete the restoration of the Byzantine Empire as the major power in the Near East and Mediterranean. The failure of this grandiose project revealed how radically the map inherited from the ancient world had changed. It showed that Constantinople was no longer capable of performing a unifying role. Islam was developing into a fully fledged civilization infinitely more impressive than Byzantium, while the papacy was able to cast off the tutelage of Constantinople and was evolving as the effective centre of Western Christendom. At the same time, the work of Maximos the Confessor was stamping the religious life of Byzantium with its distinctive traits.

Constantine IV bequeathed his son an apparently favourable situation. Shortly before Constantine died, the new caliph, 'Abd al-Malik (685–705), agreed to pay the tribute previously agreed by Mu'awiya, which the Byzantine chroniclers put at the considerable sum of 1,000 nomismata a day, which would amount to over 5,000 pounds of gold a year. These terms were then renegotiated with Justinian II. The tribute remained the same, but the Byzantine ruler agreed to evacuate the Mardaites from Syria and Cilicia, where they

50

had been such a menace to the caliphate. This was part of an attempt to create a clearly defined frontier between Byzantium and Islam, which might protect Asia Minor. A neutral zone was created stretching from the island of Cyprus to Armenia and Iberia. The revenues of these territories were to be shared equally between Byzantium and the caliphate. Justinian II has been criticized for this action on the grounds that he forfeited the initiative along the eastern frontier. In the short term, however, it gave him a free hand to concentrate on the Balkans, where Thessaloniki had long been cut off from Constantinople by the surrounding Slav tribes. In 688 he led a punitive expedition that relieved Thessaloniki and brought it more firmly under imperial control. He rounded up large numbers of Slavs and settled them in Anatolia as military colonists. The success of this policy of transfer of populations remains a matter of debate. Some of the Slavs revolted and went over to the Muslims. In reprisal, Justinian massacred others, but the overall effect was likely to have strengthened the population of north-western Anatolia, where the bulk of new settlement occurred.

THE COUNCIL IN TROULLO

To celebrate the achievements of the first years of his reign Justinian II convoked a General Council of the Church in 691. This is usually known as the Council in Troullo, after the audience hall in the imperial palace where it was held. Justinian looked on it as a continuation of the fifth and sixth General Councils, held in Constantinople in 553 and 680–81 respectively, whence the name Quinisext that is sometimes given to it. Justinian II was therefore able to present this council not only as a continuation of the work of his father, but also of that of his illustrious namesake. The purpose was to provide the practical and legal measures needed to complement the doctrinal work of the fifth and sixth General Councils. Because the Council in Troullo fits rather awkwardly into the run of General Councils of the Church, its importance has been not so much overlooked as misunderstood.

Though presented as a continuation of earlier work, the acts of the Council in Troullo represent an achievement of some originality. The liquidation of the Monothelete controversy in 680–81 to all intents and purposes put an end to the Christological debate that had exercised theologians since the early fifth century. It had become sterile. Religious thinking had moved on to a different plane. This was a consequence of the elaboration of an ascetic theology around the theme of 'a stairway to heaven'. Monks and ascetics had long been among the most important elements of a Christian society, but little attempt was made to rationalize why this should be. Perhaps the most important text was a guide to the ascetic life entitled *The Heavenly Ladder*, written in the early seventh century by St John Climax, a monk of Sinai. At exactly the same time came the first efforts to defend the use of icons, the veneration of which was becoming central to worship within the Byzantine church. In other words, the focus of religious thinking was shifting from the problem of the incarnation to the problem of the 'holy', which was associated with the question of intercession and of the interaction of human and divine. Were there people or objects that provided a readier access to the divine than others? This issue had become of deeper interest with the emergence of a Christian polity, where the secular elements inherited from the Roman and Hellenistic past had been absorbed and transformed.

Maximos the Confessor is most often remembered for his opposition to Monotheletism, but this was only a small part of his theological work. His major achievement was to tackle the new themes that were emerging. He did this from a monastic standpoint. The central tenet of his theology was 'deification' or perfectability: that is, the possibility of becoming like God that was opened up to humankind by the Incarnation. It was a programme that suited monks and ascetics, and turned the monastic order into an ecclesiastical elite.

Maximos's greatest intellectual debt was to Pseudo-Dionysius, the thinker who came closest to catching the essentials of the Byzantine thought-world with his insistence on hierarchy, harmony, and reflection. This mysterious figure, who purported to be St Paul's Athenian disciple, Dionysius the Areopagite, was writing at the turn of the fifth century, but was either ignored or treated with suspicion. It was Maximos the Confessor's achievement to bring his thought into the mainstream of orthodoxy. Pseudo-Dionysius situated the Christian message within a cosmic framework. Given that the order created by this message was in some way a reflection of the divine, Pseudo-Dionysius's ability to explain the connection was invaluable. His explanation revolved around his concept of a cosmic hierarchy, uniting heaven and earth, which, he claimed, 'causes its members to be images of God in all respects, to be clear and spotless mirrors reflecting the glow of primordial light and indeed of God himself'. In this world the focus of the hierarchical system was the liturgy, the cosmic significance of which Pseudo-Dionysius explained in his *On the ecclesiastical hierarchy*. This was an emphasis that Maximos the Confessor adopted. His *Mystagogia* was consciously a development of Pseudo-Dionysius's work on the liturgy. At one level Maximos was quite happy to present the liturgy as a re-enactment of Christ's life and sacrifice; this was an interpretation that the ordinary run of believers could grasp. But at another level the liturgy was the key to the approach to God. It allowed the participants to empty themselves of earthly passions and give themselves to the 'blessed passion of Holy Love', which would illuminate their soul in its search for God. This mystical understanding of the Eucharist was a guide for a spiritual elite, which was largely, perhaps exclusively, drawn from the monastic order.

Maximos's theology had profound implications for the ordering of society. Its emphasis on a monastic elite challenged the role of the emperor as the arbiter of society. Maximos refused to accept that the emperor had any role to play in the fixing of dogma. This was one of his reasons for opposing the Monothelete formula set out in imperial edicts. This denial by Maximos of any role for an emperor in matters of faith may explain the strange fact that the Council of 680–81 never once mentioned him, despite his opposition to Monotheletism. It would have diminished the emperor's role as the defender of orthodoxy to cite the work of Maximos.

The Council in Troullo insisted on the emperor's central role. Justinian II used it to legislate for a Christian society. Areas of life – magic, prostitution, marriage, forms of piety, the status and behaviour of the clergy – which Justinian I had regulated through imperial legislation, were now to be the business of a General Council of the Church. To assume, as many have, that this is evidence of the way in which Justinian II happily subordinated imperial power to ecclesiastical authority is wide of the mark. It is at odds with the autocratic character of the man. Using a General Council of the Church to legislate for the everyday concerns of a Christian society was a radical departure. It seems safe to accept that the initiative came from Justinian II. The Byzantine church was singularly devoid of outstanding personalities at the time. Everything points to Justinian II realizing that a *basileus* – a Christian king – should rule through the church rather than on his own account. It was a caesaro-papist programme; it envisaged a new Israel ruled over by a new David.

In keeping with the new dispensation, the new Israel had to be purged of Jewish and pagan customs that lingered on. The symbols of Christianity were not to be demeaned. The cross was not to be placed on thresholds, where it might be trodden on, but should be at eye level so that it could be properly venerated. Even more interesting, Christ was to be depicted in human form. To show him in symbolic form was to demean his humanity and the mystery of the Incarnation. This was a measure that was directed against Latin

Christianity, where it was normal to show Christ as the paschal lamb. The anti-Latin bias of the council was a direct result of a desire to impose as normative the practice of the church of Constantinople. The council rehearsed the latter's privileges and insisted on its legal equality with the church of Rome. Various Latin customs, such as clerical celibacy and fasting on Saturdays in Lent, were condemned. By way of protest Pope Sergius I (687–701) refused to sign the acts of the Council in Troullo. Justinian II ordered his arrest, but in the face of general support for the Pope the Byzantine exarch backed down. In any case, Justinian II was himself deposed in 695. When he was restored to power in 705 he was less high-handed in his treatment of the papacy. In 711 Pope Constantine journeyed to Byzantium, where he was reconciled with Justinian.

The Council in Troullo not only revealed a pattern of confrontation and reconciliation between Byzantium and Rome, it also underlined Justinian II's efforts, however vain they proved, to restore imperial unity around Constantinople. The pattern of Byzantine history throughout the seventh century was one of Constantinople surmounting a succession of crises and recovering a semblance of authority over the main provinces of the old Roman Empire. This had long taken the practical form of working through the different patriarchates. Their representatives met at the General Council of the Church, which therefore served to proclaim that, despite everything, the new Roman order still existed with its essential unity intact. How far removed this was from reality was made plain by the political collapse of the Byzantine Empire that followed Justinian II's deposition and exile to the Crimea in 695.

The most serious setback was the Muslim conquest of the exarchate of Carthage in 698. Although Byzantium held on stubbornly in Sicily, the loss of Carthage effectively put an end to the Mediterranean empire created by Justinian I. It contributed to the deterioration of the political situation at Constantinople, as one emperor followed another in quick succession, including Justinian, who was able to regain the throne in 705. The other emperors were provincial military governors, convinced that only control of the capital would secure their position and the interests of their men.

The political turmoil of the time was an offshoot of the emergence, since the reign of Heraclius, of the so-called armies of the themes. To meet the challenge of Islam, Anatolia was divided into a series of military commands. The army of the East, or the Anatolics, was quartered in south-eastern Anatolia surveying the invasion routes across the Taurus mountains; the army of Armenia, or the Armeniacs, held north-eastern Anatolia; while the strategic reserve, the Obsequium – Hellenized into Opsikion – commanded the approaches to Constantinople. The establishment of these military commands was one of those makeshift measures that become permanent. The military governor, or *strategos*, took over the administration of his area of command, while he recruited more and more of his troops locally. The theme system, as it is called, is always held to be a major strength of medieval Byzantium. It is supposed to have provided a local system of defence that saved Anatolia from the Muslims and in due course allowed the recovery of the Balkans from the Slav tribes that had settled there. In the early eighth century, however, it was more of a liability, as the different armies struggled to secure Constantinople. Against this background of political instability the Arab armies were able to raid deeper and deeper into Anatolia. It was now a dubious honour to aspire to the imperial throne. In 715 the soldiers of the Opsikion theme rebelled. The man they chose to be their emperor fled into the nearest mountains rather than accept their proposition, but he was hauled back and proclaimed emperor against his will. The Arabs were massing for another siege of Constantinople and the city's chances of survival looked slim.

Chapter Four

THE FORGING OF ISLAMIC CULTURE

Justinian II's first reign was a point of balance. He maintained the illusion of the continuing unity of the Roman world around Constantinople, but his failures pointed to the emergence of three very different medieval civilizations. In many ways Byzantium turned out to be the weakest of the medieval civilizations, with the least to offer in terms of originality and development. This was, however, counterbalanced by its ability to overcome crises and to survive, which suggests inner reserves of strength. These were mobilized by the cult of the Mother of God, which gave the society of the capital great cohesion in times of crisis.

COINS AS PROPAGANDA

The victory over Islam in 678 gave Justinian II a false idea of Byzantium's strength and influence. The Council in Troullo was designed as a celebration of its universalist claims, as was Justinian II's reform of the iconography of the Byzantine gold coinage, which was understood to be hostile to Islam. Since the turn of the sixth century it had been usual to place the head of the reigning emperor or emperors on the obverse of the coin and a cross in some form or other on the reverse. Justinian II's early issues are of this kind, but these gave way to gold coins that showed Christ on the obverse with the legend *Rex regnantium*, King of kings; on the reverse was the emperor holding a cross with the legend *servus Christi*, servant of Christ. Coins were an essential medium of royal and imperial propaganda. The legends on Justinian II's gold coinage contain the clearest statement of Byzantine imperial ideology as it had developed since the sixth century. In no way was Justinian II demeaning imperial authority; quite the reverse. It was a clear illustration of what the title *basileus* entailed in ideological terms. The *basileus* was the servant of Christ. As such, he was responsible for exercising care over Christ's dominions, which, as the title King of Kings suggested, extended throughout the *oikoumene* – the civilized world – including the lands now occupied by Islam.

This was exactly how the Umayyad caliph 'Abd al-Malik (685–705) understood the reform. Under the year 691–2 the chronicler Theophanes informs us that the Caliph sent coinage with a new type of stamp by way of payment of the tribute owed to the Byzantine Empire. Justinian refused to accept it. Equally, the Caliph made it clear that he could not accept the circulation of Byzantine coins in his dominions. He knew that his Christian subjects pointed to the Byzantine emperor's image on the coinage and used it as proof of his continuing authority over the lands of Islam. Thus began what André Grabar, the historian of iconoclasm, has called '*la guerre des symboles*' between Byzantium and Islam. This was a struggle by Islam to find a religious vocabulary to express its pre-eminence at the expense of the older power. It was a struggle in which coins played a large part, certainly at the beginning. Early Muslim coinage was largely modelled on Byzantine issues, but sanitized by having the arm of the cross removed. Experiments with coins showing Muslim symbols, such as the lance of the Prophet, were not satisfactory. But Justinian II's new iconography, with its claim to the imperialism of Christ, was a challenge to Islam, which 'Abd al-Malik took up. By 696–7 he had evolved what was to be the standard Muslim coinage to the present day. Obverse and reverse showed the basic Koranic texts. It was one of the first demonstrations of the power of Arabic calligraphy.

This reform of the coinage was part of the attempt, begun by 'Abd al-Malik and continued by his successors, to create a specifically Muslim system of images that would challenge that elaborated by Byzantium. It might seem from today's perspective that by the late seventh century Byzantium was played out and was no kind of a threat to a rampant Islam. That is not how it would have appeared at the time. Beneath the surface of Islam's conquests, which had already spread almost halfway round the world, there was a brittle and ramshackle polity. It was not unlike other nomad empires, which have tended to collapse almost as swiftly as they have arisen, absorbed by their conquered peoples. 'Abd al-Malik seems to have realized that, if Islam were to retain its distinctive character, it had to develop a politico-religious culture and ideology just as sophisticated as those of its major opponent, which was still Byzantium. His programme was sparked off by the challenge presented by Justinian II.

THE GHASSANIDS AND THE UMAYYADS

Under 'Abd al-Malik and his son al-Walid (705–15) Islam emerged as a distinct civilization. Arabic replaced Greek as the language of administration. It was the culmination of a process that had started before Muhammad first began to preach his message. Superficially at least, the Muslim conquests of the Fertile Crescent conformed to an age-old pattern that saw Arab tribes from the centre or south of the peninsula move into these lands. There was initial disruption, followed by a degree of assimilation. The previous movement of this kind occurred at the beginning of the sixth century, when the Ghassanids had moved into the fringes of the Syrian desert. They became clients of Byzantium and converted to Christianity. Justinian used them to guard his desert frontier and to shadow their opposite numbers, the Lakhmids, who were long established clients of the Sassanians.

The Ghassanids controlled the frontier from Resafa, just south of the Euphrates, to Bosra, in the lands beyond the Jordan. Resafa was a substantial city in the sixth century, one of the major centres of the cult of Saints Sergius and Bacchus, which the Ghassanids promoted. Outside its city walls the Ghassanids had their audience hall, where their chiefs received their clients. Their main residence was much further south, close to Damascus, on the Golan Heights. Supervision of such a large area meant that the Ghassanids had to be for ever on the move, but they were not, strictly speaking, nomadic. They were great builders and patrons of churches and monasteries. Despite their conversion to Christianity, they never forgot their Arab roots or culture. Along with their rivals, the Lakhmids, they were the major patrons of Arab poets, who praised their generosity and way of life. Poetry was fundamental to pre-Islamic Arab culture; it was the poets who set the tone of Arab society. The centres of Arab culture at the end of the sixth century were, therefore, to be found on the edges of the Fertile Crescent at courts that were conversant with Byzantine culture and the Sassanian court. The early success of Islam can be explained, in part, by the ease with which it was able to replace the culture of the Ghassanids and the Lakhmids. In this the Umayyads were a significant factor.

The Umayyads were a family from Mecca who, in the aftermath of the Muslim conquest, came to dominate Syria, where they made Damascus their capital. It was a city they knew well: they already had property there before the Muslim conquest. They were powerful enough to challenge the Prophet's son-in-law, Ali, for the caliphate, or headship, of Islam. Their leader, Mu'awiya (661–80), emerged victorious from this struggle and became caliph in 661. The caliphate remained in the family until the coming of the Abbasids in the mid-eighth century. The Umayyads' responsibilities as caliph determined their public face, but their private lifestyle owed much to the Ghassanids. It was seen most clearly in their 'desert palaces', which is something of a misnomer because they were, at best, only on the edge of the desert and were often the centres of agricultural enterprises, in which irrigation was an important element. The dominant feature was the audience hall. It was part of the way Umayyad princes managed their clients, most important of whom were the tribes that had been settled along the desert fringes of Syria in the wake of the Muslim conquest. The decoration of their desert palaces, a fusion of Byzantine and Sassanian techniques and motifs of great sophistication, was designed in part to show off princely power and to celebrate a princely lifestyle. The Umayyads' adoption, via the Ghassanids, of princely art and architecture was part of an experiment to create an ambience that suited their ambitions and their achievements. It may have earned them a bad reputation, but a hedonistic lifestyle was to remain a feature of Muslim princely culture, in marked contrast with the austerity of Islam.

The Umayyads never forgot that they were the leaders of a religious movement. They understood the need to create an art and architecture that would help to identify and to define Islam. The Muslim consciousness of their role as the bearers of a new and more complete revelation is evident from the way that they liked their places of worship, or mosques, to be untainted by contact with earlier places of worship. Muslims were not, at first, inclined to take over churches and convert them into mosques. They preferred to build from scratch. Churches were, in any case, the wrong shape and on the wrong alignment. They were the wrong shape because the early Christian liturgy was dominated by procession, whereas Muslim liturgy was simpler and devoted to prayer. It required a large, broad hall that in the early days could ideally accommodate the whole Muslim community. The *qibla*, or direction of prayer, meant, in addition, that the mosque had to be aligned with Mecca and not simply to the east in the manner of Christian churches. The early mosques that were constructed in the great camps of Islam at Fustat,

Kufa, and Basra were arranged along the *qibla* side of an enclosed space and were simple halls. They took as their model the House of the Prophet at Medina. In its original form it was a large walled space with a lean-to along one side. It was a place where the Prophet's followers could gather. The mosque became increasingly elaborate as Muslims in the newly conquered territories started to make use of the building techniques and architectural features that they found there.

Until the reign of 'Abd al-Malik the Umayyads seem to have paid little attention to providing the Muslims of Syria with appropriate religious buildings. This was in part because the circumstances of the conquest had meant that there were relatively few Muslims settled in Syria. The Christians had surrendered on terms that had allowed them to keep their cities and places of worship, and as yet there were relatively few conversions to Islam. Egyptian papyri reveal that the Islamic conquest initially changed very little in terms of administration and taxation. This was the case in Syria too: it remained a preponderantly Christian society and the early Umayyads relied very heavily on Christian administrators. Thus, paradoxically, the Umayyad capital of Damascus remained a Christian city. When the Frankish pilgrim Arculf visited Damascus in the early 680s he was impressed by the harmony that existed between Christian and Muslim, and noted that the former allowed the latter a space for prayer in the Cathedral of John the Baptist. Arculf described Jerusalem as still an entirely Christian city.

THE DOME OF THE ROCK

This period of *convivencia* came to an end in the aftermath of the Umayyad defeat beneath the walls of Constantinople in 678. The activities of the Mardaites revealed how vulnerable the Muslim hold on Syria was, and the pretentious claims of Justinian II underlined how rudimentary Islam still was in political and ideological terms.

In the great Muslim camps, which were the motors of Muslim conquest, the message of the Prophet was sufficient. In Syria the Umayyads felt isolated in a Christian society set amidst splendid monuments that proclaimed its message. 'Abd al-Malik sought to refashion Islam to meet the challenge of Christianity. We have seen how he changed the administrative language from Greek to Arabic and created a specifically Muslim coinage. These measures were complemented by the symbolic appropriation of the land, starting with the holy city of Jerusalem. It was still dominated by the Church of the Holy Sepulchre and the adjacent Anastasis Rotunda, which was supposed to mark Christ's grave. On the other side of the city Mount Moriah, the site of the Jewish temple, had been cleared by Caliph Mu'awiya and then abandoned. 'Abd al-Malik appropriated it in order to build the Dome of the Rock, which was completed by 691–2. This was not a mosque but a commemorative building, intended to celebrate Muhammad's night journey. It was a way of infusing Jerusalem with a clearer Islamic significance. Mount Moriah, or the Temple Rock, was originally associated with Abraham. Its new association with Muhammad's night journey emphasized the claim that Islam was the true religion of Abraham, which the Jews had distorted. At the same time the Temple Rock came to be associated with Muslim traditions about the last days, when paradise would be transferred to Jerusalem and the Gate of Paradise would open up above the city. The entrances of the Dome of the Rock – the Gate of the Angel and the Gate of Paradise – refer to these traditions. An early tradition of the Prophet has Allah proclaiming: 'This is the place of my throne on the day of the resurrection of the dead and the gathering of my servants.' There were suspicions that 'Abd al-Malik was trying to turn Jerusalem into the new focus of Islam at the expense of Mecca. It is true that at the time that construction on the Dome of the Rock began Mecca was in the hands of rivals of the Umayyads. 'Abd al-Malik even put an embargo on the pilgrimage to Mecca. Competition with Mecca may have played a small part in his decision to erect the Dome of the Rock on the site of the Jewish temple, but more urgent was the need to stamp Islam's authority on the holy city.

The Dome of the Rock was constructed as a counterpoint to the Anastasis Rotunda; their dimensions were almost identical and their architecture very similar. The Dome of the Rock conformed to the pattern of late antique commemorative buildings: it was domed and circular. As such, it belongs much more to the architecture of late antiquity than it does to that of Islam. It was part of the Umayyad experiment, which sought to harness the art and architecture of late antiquity to the needs of a new faith. This can be seen very clearly in the decoration. It made use of floral and vegetal motifs interspersed with vases and cornucopia in the usual late antique manner. There were new features too: jewels and crowns were concentrated around the inner sanctuary, symbols of the triumph of Islam, but more important were the Koranic texts, which proclaimed the mission and the superiority of Islam. The Dome of the Rock contained a challenge to submit to Islam. While its architecture represents the end of a tradition, the decoration pointed the way forward to the non-representational art of Islam, where the accent is on calligraphy.

'Abd al-Malik's son and successor, al-Walid (705–15), completed his father's work on the Temple Rock by constructing the Aqsa Mosque adjacent to it. It was intended as a single complex. This mosque, too, commemorated Muhammad's night journey. It stood in relation to the Dome of the Rock in much the same way as the Church of the Holy Sepulchre did to the Anastasis Rotunda. The original decoration of the Aqsa Mosque has not survived and the mosque has been much rebuilt, but the basic plan testifies to the elaboration of mosque architecture associated with the work of al-Walid, as features from Byzantine architecture were incorporated. The main axis was emphasized by a raised gable above the main entrance and by a dome over the *mihrab* bay, which was the focal point of the interior of the mosque because it indicated the direction of prayer. Though the elements were Byzantine, the reformulation of their function produced a new architecture.

THE GREAT MOSQUE AT DAMASCUS

In addition to the Aqsa Mosque, al-Walid was responsible for rebuilding the House of the Prophet at Medina and the Great Mosque at Damascus. We are told that for these projects al-Walid requested aid from the Byzantine emperor. To help with the reconstruction of the House of the Prophet and the Great Mosque at Damascus the emperor sent a tribute of gold, as well as craftsmen and loads of mosaic cubes. Nothing is said about help for the Umayyad constructions on the Temple Rock, but the Dome of the Rock was certainly the work of architects and craftsmen brought up in the best Byzantine traditions. Al-Walid will have regarded the Byzantine contribution to his building projects as a sign of their client status; the Byzantine emperor will have regarded it, with less justice, as an exercise in largesse. It was a point of balance. The need for Byzantine assistance confirms that Constantinople remained the centre to which its political successors still looked for artistic expertise. But it was only a moment. Thereafter Muslim rulers would have little need of Byzantium. Before too long, as we shall see, Byzantine emperors would be looking to Muslim courts for the latest styles.

Al-Walid's most ambitious and costly project was the Great Mosque at Damascus. It cost him seven years' tax revenue from Syria, not to mention eighteen ships' loads of gold and silver from Cyprus and whatever the Byzantine emperor contributed. Al-Walid had first to buy the Cathedral of John the Baptist from the Christian community. He promptly pulled it down, leaving only the walled enclosure, which dated back to the original occupant of the site, a temple of Zeus. It measured some 150 by 100 yards. Al-Walid had three of its sides lined with colonnades, while the mosque was constructed along the south wall. It took the shape of three long aisles parallel to the wall. Cutting across them was the main axis of the building, which was marked by a gabled transept with a dome over the *mihrab* bay. Once again Byzantine features were put at the service of Islam. This was equally true of its mosaic decoration, which still constitutes the chief glory of the Great Mosque. It shows a paradisiacal landscape of trees, rivers, mills, and villas, but human figures are conspicuously absent. It was the final – and perhaps greatest – flowering of the illusionist landscape of antiquity. It counts as the most ambitious creation of the Umayyad experiment. Within a few decades of completion it was being hailed as one of the wonders of the world, but, unlike the decoration of the Dome of the Rock, it was to have no future. Later Muslim writers did not quite know what to make of it. Modern scholars are in no doubt that it is a depiction of paradise, but are less sure whether it is paradise on earth or paradise to come. There seems no reason why it should not be both, the one being a distant reflection of the other. Through their rule the Umayyads could claim to be creating paradise on earth as they extended the House of Islam, which was only a foretaste of the greater delights that awaited the true believer. The theme of paradise was entirely appropriate to the moment. After the setbacks in the late seventh century Islam was once again rampant. Carthage and North Africa had been conquered and the armies of Islam were pouring into Spain. In 714 al-Walid and his court assembled in the newly completed Great Mosque to fête the Muslim conqueror of North Africa. The Great Mosque proclaimed the triumph of Islam to both the Christians of Syria and the Byzantines.

FIGURES, SYMBOLS, AND CALLIGRAPHY

There were to be no imitators, because Muslim taste in religious art was hardening. There was less and less room for naturalism, even in the comparatively innocuous form it took in the Great Mosque.

The Koran has little to say about art. There were traditions that when Muhammad cleansed the shrine of the Ka'ba at Mecca of idols, he made an exception for images of Christ and his mother. In its earliest years Islam was indifferent to figurative art; iconoclasm was not built into Islam from the outset. Distrust of figurative art was a corollary of a specifically Islamic artistic vocabulary. While the Koran is reticent about art, it extols calligraphy: 'Recite! Your Lord is the most bountiful one, who by the pen taught man what he did not know' (Sura 96.1). The traditions of the Prophet built upon this. They described calligraphy as 'a spiritual geometry, wrought by a material instrument'. Tradition had it that Muhammad enjoined 'beauty of handwriting ... for it is one of the keys of man's daily bread'. It was entirely appropriate that texts from the Koran should become a dominant feature of Muslim religious art. The Koran was, after all, the word of God. This was in marked contrast to Christianity, where it was Christ himself who was the word of God. One of the major arguments in favour of religious images put forward by Christian apologists was that they were a way of bearing witness to the Incarnation. The religious symbolism that Islam and Christianity evolved reflected their essential teachings about the nature of divine revelation. Once Islam began to evolve its own religious art, it became increasingly difficult for Muslims to accept figurative art for religious purposes. This is reflected in the traditions of the Prophet as they developed over the course of the eighth century. One of the best known concerns the Last Judgement, where painters would be challenged to breathe life into their creations. When they failed, they would be punished for eternity for their presumption in seeking to usurp God's creative function. This Muslim tradition was known to Theodore Abu-Qurra, a Syrian Christian theologian writing in the late eighth century. He was trying to defend the veneration of images, which Christian congregations were beginning to abandon in the face of Muslim disapproval. This is very different from John of Damascus, whose tract against Islam, written nearer the beginning of the century, contains not a hint about Muslim criticism of Christian veneration of icons. The hardening of attitudes occurred quite suddenly. It can be traced in the growing Muslim hostility to Christian symbols, the start of which coincided with 'Abd al-Malik's confrontation with Justinian II. Muslims found the cross most offensive. As early as 689 the governor of Egypt ordered the destruction of crosses, which culminated in a general ban on the public display of the cross. This led to the sporadic attacks on images. Under Yazid II (720–24) there was a general destruction of figurative imagery, which can be documented in the churches and synagogues of Syria and Palestine.

The reigns of 'Abd al-Malik and al-Walid saw the crystallization of an Islamic art and architecture, which proclaimed a new religion and a new civilization. Many of its basic elements derived from Byzantium but they would be utterly transformed by the need to create an art and architecture that suited its religious needs. It was a time of experiment and there was much that would be discarded. Religion was the dynamic element, but the creative process was spurred on by the challenge from Christianity, whether in the shape of Christian communities under Muslim rule or in the form of the Christian polity of Byzantium. These were united in the Church Councils held in Constantinople in 680–81 and 691–2, where representatives of the patriarchate of Jerusalem had a prominent role to play. The power of the General Council of the Church was celebrated in the mosaics of the Church of the Nativity at Bethlehem. It gave the illusion that despite the Muslim conquests the unity of the Christian world still held firm. It was in this spirit that Justinian II made his presumptuous demands. Islam needed to demonstrate its power and independence in ways that Christianity could understand. In the face of this challenge it soon became clear how weak Byzantium was. Even ecclesiastical solidarity proved something of a mirage.

The Umayyad experiment turned into a triumphant celebration

of Islam. It did seem possible, as Muslim armies stood poised at the passes of the Pyrenees and at the gates of Constantinople, that the Umayyads might possibly reconstitute the unity of the old Roman world in a new Islamic guise. The Islamic achievement was, in some ways, still more remarkable, since its orbit encompassed so much greater a span than the Roman Empire. However, both Byzantium and Latin Christendom were able to defy Islam and to create barriers, physical and psychological, that protected them against Muslim pre-eminence, Islam had created a distinctive and, in almost every respect, superior civilization. Latin Christendom was far enough removed from the main centres of Islam to ignore the threat it posed. For Byzantium it was different. The success of Islam destroyed its claims to universal authority. This struck at the heart of the Byzantine identity created in the aftermath of Constantine's conversion to Christianity. For much of the seventh century Byzantium survived by being in denial. But this could not be maintained indefinitely. In 717 the Muslim armies descended once again on Constantinople. The Byzantine Empire seemed on the point of extinction, but managed to survive. This was largely due to the abilities of a new emperor, who set about restoring the empire, but this time in full recognition of the power of Islam.

Chapter Five

BYZANTINE ICONOCLASM

B yzantium seemed to be a lost cause in the opening years of
the eighth century. Its people seemed more interested in their
own political rivalries than in confronting the enemy. In 715,
in the face of yet another rebellion, the emperor of the day abandoned Constantinople and retired to the greater safety of Thessaloniki. Byzantine morale was so poor that in one provincial city
the people resorted to sacrificing a baby to hold back the Muslims.
The first line of defence should have been provided by the army of
the Anatolic theme, but its governor, a Syrian called Leo, better
known as Leo III (717–41), came to terms with the Muslims. With
their connivance, Leo was able to secure Constantinople and the
crown, but failed to keep his side of the bargain. Instead of sur-
rendering the city, he conducted a defence of great bravery. The
Arabs were beaten by the summer of 718, when the siege was called
off. Once again the Mother of God received the credit. This victory
was not followed by any political collapse on the part of the Umayyad
caliphate, as had occurred after the previous siege of Constantinople.
Instead, the armies of Islam remained a formidable force throughout
Leo III's reign. The attacks on Anatolia continued. In 726 the
Muslims were able to lay siege to the city of Nicaea, less than a
hundred miles from Constantinople.

EMPEROR VERSUS PATRIARCH

Leo III may have saved Constantinople from the Arabs, but his empire was in a fearful state. Anatolia was vulnerable. The previous emperor still held Thessaloniki, and Sicily was in revolt. Leo III dealt with the rebels in the ruthless manner that marked his style of rule. The former emperor was brought from Thessaloniki along with the archbishop. Leo had both executed and their heads paraded through the hippodrome during a celebration of the races. The Sicilian rebellion was suppressed with equal resolution. The Arabs were beaten off from Nicaea. Gradually the tide along the eastern frontier began to turn in Byzantium's favour.

Leo III followed these early successes by imposing more direct control over the provinces in the form of some reorganization of the theme system and the reassessment of taxes. This produced a serious rebellion around the Aegean in 727. The rebels commandeered elements of the fleet and launched an assault on Constantinople, which was beaten off. In Sicily and the remaining Italian territories Leo's measures not only produced heavier taxation, but also involved the confiscation of papal estates in Sicily. In return the papacy fomented considerable unrest. Leo III countered by transferring ecclesiastical jurisdiction over Sicily and southern Italy – Rome's metropolitan diocese – and over Illyricum, which included Thessaloniki, from Rome to Constantinople. This action remained a bone of contention between the Churches of Rome and Constantinople for centuries. It also reflected an assumption that political and ecclesiastical boundaries should coincide. The universalism that had been the hallmark of the Christian Roman Empire was being abandoned. Leo III saw Byzantium as a gathered community, a new Israel. It was only by returning to its Old Testament roots that Byzantium would be able to forge a strength of purpose capable of matching that of Islam.

One feature of Leo III's restoration of the Byzantine Empire has always been singled out: his iconoclasm. The origins and character of his iconoclast policies are hard to disentangle from the web of later prejudice. It is not even certain that the Emperor would have thought of himself as an iconoclast, though his opponents certainly did. The first evidence of an iconoclast movement is found in letters written by Patriarch Germanos I (715–30) to the bishops of Claudiopolis and Nakoleia, places perched on the north-western edge of the Anatolian plateau. The Patriarch also wrote to their superior, the Metropolitan Bishop of Synada, wondering why he had not disciplined them. The letters can be dated to the mid- to late 720s. They reveal that there was considerable agitation against images in western Asia Minor. A sign of the upheaval was that the wonder-working icon of Sozopolis – the one that Theodore of Sykeon had supposedly venerated – had ceased to function. This disenchantment with images must have been connected with the demoralization produced by repeated Arab attacks, which in Anatolia did not end with the victory of 718. There was a telling episode from the Arab siege of Nicaea in 726, when a Byzantine soldier hurled a stone at an icon of the Mother of God. It was symptomatic of the way icons had singularly failed to protect the people of Asia Minor from the ravages of the Muslims. The Patriarch assumed something rather different: that the outbreak of iconoclasm was a reaction to Muslim criticism. He reminded the Bishop of Nakoleia that the Muslims might criticize icons as idolatrous, but what did they do? They worshipped a stone!

The Byzantines were sensitive to Muslim criticisms. At the time of the siege of Constantinople, or possibly shortly afterwards, Leo III and Caliph Umur II (717–20) exchanged letters. The Caliph criticized Christian veneration of both the cross and images. The Emperor angrily rejected criticism of the former, but admitted that images did not deserve the same respect, 'not having received in Holy Scripture any commandment whatsoever in their regard'. However, this did not mean that images were to be discarded; they served a useful function as a memorial and as an aid to worship. The Emperor concluded: '. . . but as for the wood and the colours, we do not give them any reverence'. This was the signal for an attack on the Muslim practice of venerating the Ka'ba, the most sacred shrine at Mecca. The Emperor's ideas about images do not seem at this stage all that far removed from those of his patriarch. It was clear, however, that in the face of Muslim criticism he assigned them an inferior role by comparison with the cross. Behind iconoclasm was a recognition of Islam's overwhelming success.

Leo III was sensitive to any agitation in western Anatolia. It was the powerhouse of the military organization. A significant proportion of the key fortresses and theme headquarters were concentrated in the area. The need to arrive at some solution was made all the more urgent in 726 by the spectacular explosion of the volcanic island of Santorini in the Aegean. It was a sign: the seas round about started to boil and pumice stone from the eruption was deposited from Crete to the shores of western Asia Minor. Patriarch Germanos I was not sympathetic to the iconoclast agitation that ensued. He proceeded against the Bishop of Nakoleia. Leo III took the Bishop under imperial protection and demanded a proper ruling on the veneration of images. The Patriarch argued that this was the business of a General Council of the Church. Leo III took matters into his own hands: he convened the imperial council on 7 January 730 and enacted a decree against icons. The Patriarch resigned ten days later. The exact wording of the decree has not been preserved and the nature of Leo's iconoclasm is therefore hard to pinpoint. It may have been quite anodyne, designed mostly to end the extravagances of image veneration, which in some cases imbued the icon with magical powers. It was certainly designed to emphasize the cross as the symbol of Christian victory, and it does seem likely that Leo III replaced the image of Christ above the Chalke Gate with a cross. Despite later fabrications, there was very little in the way of opposition to Leo III's measure and very little in the way of persecution.

That Leo III had a high conceit of the imperial office is nevertheless apparent from his assertion in a letter to a pope that he was both priest and emperor. His meaning becomes clearer when we consider his major achievement. This was the law code known as the *Ekloga*, issued in 741, the last year of his reign. Its intention was in the first instance practical: it was designed to provide a legal handbook that would raise the standard and effectiveness of provincial administration. Much of it was a précis of Justinianic law, but Christian influence was apparent in the divorce laws and in the substitution of mutilation for the death penalty. Its flavour was biblical. Its social teaching can be traced back to Isaiah. Byzantium was the new Israel and the Emperor was the new Moses leading his people to salvation. In the preface the Emperor also likens himself to St Peter, for in the same way as the apostle, he had been called by Christ to feed his flock. He meant by this that he should nurture a Christian society through good government. Leo III reasserted the codification of the laws as an imperial prerogative and abandoned Justinian II's experiment of legislating through a General Council of the Church. This can best be explained by the isolation of Byzantium from the other Christian Churches, which is apparent in their criticism of the Emperor's iconoclast policies. Leo's comparison of his responsibilities to those of St Peter would not have pleased the papacy. Pope Gregory II (715–31) was among the sternest critics of his treatment of Germanos I. The Pope's successor and namesake called a council at Rome in 731 and condemned Leo III's edict against images. It marked a further step in the separation of Rome and Constantinople.

JOHN OF DAMASCUS

The bitterest criticism of Leo III came from a different quarter, from John of Damascus, who had become a monk in the Monastery of the Great Lavra of St Sabas outside Jerusalem. When and why he launched his attack on Leo III remain matters of speculation. It is most likely that he had been alerted to Leo's iconoclasm by Rome's condemnation of the Emperor in 731. Given that relations between the Churches of Rome and Jerusalem were very close at the time, it seems most unlikely that Rome's condemnation would not have been communicated to the church of Jerusalem.

John of Damascus's defence of images put the controversy on a new intellectual footing. Its starting point was the argument that an icon of Christ was testimony to the Incarnation. But the Incarnation not only made possible the depiction of Christ, it also sanctified matter. John took great care to show that venerating an icon of Christ did not therefore mean worshipping matter. He was very clear that worship went to the 'God of matter ... who worked out my salvation through matter'. As a result, matter is to be honoured but not worshipped. This applied to the materials out of which an icon was made. This was a far cry from the idolatry of pagans. The important point was, in any case, not the materials, but the likeness produced, which ensured a relative identity between the image and the original. This helped the viewer to raise his or her thoughts to higher things, thus opening up the path to mysteries. It was a demonstration that the image partook, to however limited a degree, of the power and virtue of the original.

This argument could be extended from an icon of Christ to an icon of his mother, the Theotokos, given her role in the Incarnation. John of Damascus reveals that there were those who accepted the veneration of icons of Christ and the Theotokos, but rejected that of any others. He fails to identify who these people were, but this practice was a feature of early iconoclasm. It was a charge made independently against Leo III. John of Damascus took it as an attack on the cult of saints, arguing that rejection of their images disparaged the honour due to the saints. When alive, the saints had been filled with the Holy Spirit. Their virtue continued to inhere not only in their relics, but also in their icons, which preserved their likeness 'not by nature, but by grace and divine power'. John construed an attack upon icons as a rejection of the idea of intercession and of the continuation of Christ's ministry through his apostles and his saints, who were inspired by the Holy Spirit.

John of Damascus faced up to the implications of an attack upon icons. His understanding was likely to have been far more subtle than that of his opponents, who were unlikely to see the relevance of Pseudo-Dionysius's hierarchical structure of the cosmos to the question of whether or not icons should be venerated. John gave Pseudo-Dionysius's construction a new relevance by thinking in terms of a hierarchy of images, providing a chain that linked the godhead with the natural world. At the top came the natural image: that of Christ, the natural image of God the Father. Another link in the chain was an image by imitation: that of man, who was made in the image of God. Right at the bottom came the icon, which was bracketed with the written word. This would seem to be making a rather modest claim for the role of icons, but it was a most subtle defence. John was arguing that if you attacked icons, you were attacking the hierarchy of images that was integral to the Christian system of belief and worship. An attack on icons was thus tantamount to denying that Christ was the image of God the Father. John of Damascus had produced an overarching explanation of the place of images in Christianity of an imagination and power that has not been surpassed. He situated icons in the tradition of the Christian faith. He made it clear that they were to be venerated only for the likeness they showed. They were not of themselves worthy of worship – that went to the original of the figure portrayed. But this in itself meant that an attack on icons was an attack on the whole edifice of faith.

John's opponents insisted on knowing what authority validated his scheme. They would have reason to doubt that there was any support to be found in the Bible. John's answer was simple: many Christian practices had no written authority, but were part of a living tradition that was just as valid. Attack it and the church would lose its vitality. John of Damascus was convinced that an attack on icons would deprive Christianity of its substance and reduce it to the recitation of a few prayers, not unlike – though this is never stated – Islam.

What had opened up this prospect? John of Damascus identified imperial interference as the church's Achilles' heel . 'Emperors have no right to make laws in the Church', he expostulated. 'The good ordering of the state is the business of the *basileus*, ecclesiastical order is a matter for pastors and theologians. This attack amounts to an act of robbery.' The purity of the faith could be guaranteed only if the emperor were kept at an arm's length. This position owed much to Maximos the Confessor and went directly counter to the caesaro-papist agenda set out, in their different ways, by Justinian II and by Leo III and his son Constantine V. John of Damascus's attack on imperial authority meant that there could be no compromise. It was to be Emperor Constantine V who developed an iconoclast theology that went some way towards meeting John of Damascus's defence of images.

CONSTANTINE V

Constantine V's accession in 741 was traumatic. In the previous year he had helped his father defeat the Arab forces. It was a decisive victory, and it gave the Byzantines nearly forty years of peace along the eastern frontier, as the Umayyad caliphate disintegrated, to be replaced by the Abbasids. For his pains, the new emperor was hustled out of Constantinople by his brother-in-law Artavasdos, who restored the icons as the badge of his regime. Thanks to the support of the Thrakesion and Anatolic themes, Constantine recovered the capital in 743. One of his tasks was to provide an effective defence of iconoclasm. The second commandment – 'Thou shalt not make unto thyself any graven image . . .' – was no longer quite enough, even when backed up by the authority of Epiphanius of Salamis, a noted father of the church from the turn of the fourth century.

Constantine V elaborated his views in a series of *Enquiries*. He started by establishing how the image related to the original or prototype. He admitted that there were many kinds of images, but maintained that the true image must in essence be identical with the original. To support this he cited the letter written by Eusebius of Caesarea to the Emperor Constantine's sister, which made a clear distinction between an image of Christ 'which bears his essential characteristics' and a depiction of the man Jesus. Art was quite incapable of capturing the former. In that case, Constantine V argued, the true image of Christ was to be found only in the Eucharist. He also built on the notion that man was made in God's image, meaning that by imbibing the example of Christ and his saints the ordinary believer could become a reflection – an image – of their virtues. This has been termed the ethical theory of images. It was important because it opened up to the pious laity a role that had been reserved for the monastic order.

Constantine's most notorious contribution to the debate over icons was his argument about circumscribability. This brought into play the whole controversy about the nature of Christ. The argument was as follows: if you circumscribe Christ through art, you are *either* emphasizing his human nature at the expense of the divine, in the manner of the Nestorians, *or* confusing his natures, in the manner of the Monophysites. Icons consequently contradicted the church's

1. The colossal head of Constantine the Great: Palazzo dei Conservatori, Rome.

2. Constantine/Justinian mosaic: St Sophia, Istanbul. Above the south door of the narthex, most probably tenth century. It shows Constantine (right) offering the Mother of God and Child a model of the city of Constantinople, while Justinian (left) offers one of St Sophia. This mosaic presents Constantine and Justinian as the co-founders of the Byzantine Empire; Justinian's work as legislator and a builder symbolised by St Sophia giving form to Constantine's act of founding a new imperial capital.

Obelisk showing Theodosius I at games: Hippodrome, Istanbul. This relief was added to the
obelisk from Karnak that Theodosius I had erected along the central spine of the Hippodrome
Constantinople. It shows Theodosius and his family presiding over the games.

4. The city walls of Constantinople, constructed in 412 under Theodosius II. The supreme achievement of Roman military engineering, they defied all enemies until 1204.

5. Mosaic from the Rotunda, Thessaloniki. Originally the mausoleum of the pagan Emperor Galerius, it was converted in the fifth century into a Christian church. The mosaic decoration consists of a calendar of saints. Their heavenly abode is represented by an idealisation of the imperial palace.

Sts Sergius and Bacchus, Istanbul. Built by Justinian and Theodora in their palace of
ormisdas, which they occupied before ascending to the imperial dignity in 527. The combination
'experimental planning and superb architectural ornament makes it the most exciting of
stinianic buildings.

7. Interior of St Sophia, Istanbul. Gaspare and Giuseppe Fossati were the architects used by the Ottomans to restore the church in the mid-nineteenth century. Their paintings of the interior do justice to its romantic atmosphere.

8. Apse mosaic: St Catherine's, Sinai. St Catherine's was completed with help from Justinian circa 550. The apse mosaic shows the transfiguration, but presents Christ and his Apostles in human form, pointing to the existence of different currents of thought about the possibilities of representation.

9. Christ icon: St Catherine's, Sinai. Dating from the late sixth century, this is the earliest surviving example of Christ Pantokrator. It is perhaps modelled on one of the *acheiropoietai* images of Christ which became popular at the time. Christ is shown bearded, but instead of the severity associated with later Pantokrators, the artist has preferred to emphasize Christ's humanity. It reflects the argument that images of Christ were testimony to His Incarnation.

10. Ivory of Archangel Michael: British Museum, London. Dated to the mid-sixth century, it is the largest surviving Byzantine ivory and one of the most accomplished. The inscription reads: 'Receive the suppliant's petition.'

11. Justinian and his court: San Vitale, Ravenna. On the northern sanctuary wall of the church.

12. Theodora and her court: San Vitale, Ravenna. On the southern sanctuary wall of the church.

13. Madrid Skylitzes: Bibliotheca nacional, Madrid. A miniature from a twelfth-century manuscript, showing the devastating effects of Greek Fire. The inscription reads: 'The fleet of the Romans firing on an opposing fleet.'

4. The 'Ladder of Virtue' of St John Climax: St Catherine's, Sinai. A twelfth-century icon showing St John Climax's mystical ascent to the Godhead; envisaged in terms of thirty rungs of a ladder, with devils lying in wait for the unwary.

15. David Plate: Metropolitan Museum, New York. Showing David slaying Goliath. Control stamps place this set of plates in the reign of the Emperor Heraclius (610-41). This scene celebrates the emperor's victory over the Persians. The choice of Old Testament imagery underlines the theme of Byzantium as the New Israel.

6. The Dome of the Rock, Jerusalem –
exterior. Begun in 691-92 by Caliph 'Abd
l-Malik, it was designed to commemorate
Muhammad's night journey and impress the
camp of Islam on a still-Christian city.

7. The Dome of the Rock, Jerusalem –
interior. The introduction of texts from the
Koran was the most original feature of the
decoration.

18. Great Mosque, Damascus – interior. The imagery of the mosaics creates a paradisiacal atmosphere and was the last flowering of the illusionist art of antiquity.

19. Muslim calligraphy: Nishapur plate, ninth century, Victoria and Albert Museum, London. Islam found in calligraphy an original and satisfying form of decoration, making use of texts from the Koran.

20. Great Mosque, Cordoba – entrance to the mihrab. The mihrab was a prayer niche on the side of a mosque facing Mecca. It was a distinctive feature of a mosque and the focus of the building. This example dates from the middle of the tenth century and its mosaic decoration was the work of Byzantine craftsmen despatched by the Emperor Constantine VII Porphyrogenitus.

21. St Irene, Istanbul – interior. Originally built in the sixth century under Justinian, it was reconstructed after an earthquake in 740 by the Iconoclast Constantine V. Note the iconoclast cross in the apse.

. Christ in Majesty, Godescalc Evangelistiary: bliothèque Nationale, Paris. Dating to 781 this nptuous manuscript was commissioned by narlemagne to celebrate the baptism of his son pin at Rome and to thank Pope Hadrian for acting his son's godfather. It represented the high point co-operation between Charlemagne and Hadrian.

23. Reliquary statue of Ste Foy: Conques, France. The devotion to miracle-working relics in the West led to the creation of anthropomorphic reliquaries.

24. Apse mosaic: St Sophia, Istanbul. Enthroned Mother of God and Infant Christ. In his description of the apse mosaic of St Sophia the Patriarch Photios refers to a standing figure of the Mother of God, rather than an enthroned one, thus casting doubt on whether this is the actual composition inaugurated by Photios on 29 March 867.

25. Apse mosaic: the Church of the Dormition, Iznik. A standing Mother of God and Infant Christ, usually referred to as the Hodegetria. This became the standard iconography for the apse after the defeat of iconoclasm. This figure was part of the restoration of icons; the traces of an iconoclast cross can just be made out in the gold mosaic background.

26 and 27. Dome mosaic: St Sophia, Thessaloniki. Showing the Ascension, with Christ being borne aloft by two angels. Around the rim of the dome are the twelve apostles and the Mother of God between two angels. Dated by inscription to the 880s.

NYΞ   HCAIAC)

ὀρθρος

8. Paris Psalter: Bibliothèque Nationale, Paris. The Prayer of Isaiah. The prophet stands between ersonifications of Night and Dawn. This psalter is the quintessence of the Macedonian Renaissance here the techniques of classical art were put at the service of Christianity.

ϹΑΟΥΛΕΝ
ΧΗΛΗΑϹΙ
ΚΑΙΔΑΔ
ΕΝΜΥΡΙ
ΑϹΙ

ϹΑ
ΟΥΛ

29. Paris Psalter: Bibliothèque Nationale, Paris. Saul and David welcomed by the daughter of Israel.
The iconography is adapted from a classical scene showing Iphigenia among the Taurians. The
inscription reads: 'Saul in his thousands and David in his tens of thousands'.

30. Panel of Constantine Porphyrogenitus: Pushkin Museum of Fine Art, Moscow.
The Emperor Constantine Porphyrogenitus (945-59) being crowned by Christ.

31. West end: Capella Palatina, Palermo. Above the royal dais – note the two emblematic lions – is an enthroned Pantokrator flanked by St Peter and St Paul. The mosaic was added during a second stage of decoration, when – most likely – an audience chamber was converted into a palace chapel.

ɔse mosaic: Cefalù Cathedral. Only the apse and the side walls of the sanctuary were decorated in
c. The work was completed by 1148. The conch of the apse is occupied in the Norman way by a
f the Pantokrator. Below is the Mother of God flanked by angels.

33. The belfry: the Church of the Martorana, Palermo (after H. Galley Knight). It was the belfry more than any other feature of the Martorana which excited the admiration of the Muslim traveller Ibn Jubayr. Paradoxically, this was a Western addition to a church built in the Byzantine tradition.

Christological teachings, which had been hammered out at a succession of Church Councils.

By 754 Constantine felt the time had come to call a Church Council to approve his iconoclast theology. It was well attended by bishops from within the Byzantine Empire – no less than 338 came – but there were no representatives present from the other patriarchates, an indication of how iconoclasm had isolated Byzantium from the other Churches. With some minor additions, the council approved the Emperor's formulations. The support they received from the assembled bishops and monks was impressive. In part, it was a matter of loyalty to the reigning emperor. This is a theme that comes out of a dialogue of the time between an iconoclast and an iconodule, a supporter of images. The former accuses the latter of being in the wrong simply because he opposes imperial authority: was he not aware that the emperor was the 'imitator of Christ' and therefore knew best?

At the Council of 754 Constantine V provided iconoclasm, at least in a Byzantine context, with theological and ecclesiastical legitimacy. He also constructed a clear rationale of iconoclasm to counter the defence of images set out by John of Damascus. Iconoclasm was founded upon a vision of Christian society that was entirely traditional. It was built around the imperial office, which worked in conjunction with the hierarchy of bishops to instil a proper sense of order. Christian worship was to be concentrated in churches and to focus on the performance of the liturgy and the veneration of the cross. All these were properly consecrated and under the control of the ecclesiastical hierarchy. The icon was rejected because there was 'no prayer of consecration to transform it into something sacred. It therefore remained', in the words of the council, 'as worthless, as the artist made it.' Constantine V wished to ensure that power was in authorized hands. This he saw as a recipe for an ordered and disciplined society.

It is unlikely that the Council of 754 was followed by a concerted attack on religious art. Some of its measures were conciliatory. It went out of its way to honour Mary as the mother of God and stressed her intercessory role, along with that of the saints. Thus iconoclasm was carefully distancing itself from any charge that it was hostile to the cult of saints. The main change in church decoration, which was characteristic of iconoclast art, was the installation of a cross in the apse. Sometimes, as in the Church of the Dormition at Nicaea, an image of the Mother in God in the apse was replaced by a cross. At the Church of the Blachernai it seems that Constantine V had a cycle of Christ's life removed and substituted a decoration of flowers and foliage in the manner of late antiquity. But there was much that escaped immediate destruction. It was not until 767–68 that the patriarch Niketas removed figurative art from the patriarchal apartments; the crosses that were substituted can still be seen. But by this time the mood had changed and Constantine V was losing his patience with those who refused to acknowledge the Council of 754. He had one monk whipped to death for denouncing him as another Julian the Apostate and a new Valens, which can only have reinforced the reputation he was gaining as a persecutor.

His major opponent in monastic circles was a hermit called Stephen, later canonized as St Stephen the Younger. As a young man Stephen established himself on Mount Auxentius, which lies across the Sea of Marmora from Constantinople and is in easy touch with the capital. He built up a reputation for holiness and was consulted on spiritual matters by members of the Constantinopolitan elite. Monastic leaders who were summoned to attend the Council of 754 went to seek his advice. Stephen suggested they should boycott the council and, if need be, flee the land. It was only after the Council had broken up that the Emperor got wind of Stephen's influence. He sent one of his agents to obtain Stephen's signature to the acts of the council. Despite considerable pressure, Stephen refused. If for no other reason, he could hardly acquiesce in the anathema launched by the council against Patriarch Germanos, for he had been baptized by Germanos and always held him in the highest reverence. From then on Stephen was a marked man. But Constantine would have preferred to win him over, in the same way that he was able to win over other monastic leaders. He failed. Finally on 28 November 765 the saint was thrown to the mob, who beat him to death. Stephen was not alone in his resistance. In jail he came across other monks who had been imprisoned for their resistance to the Council of 754. The superficial point at issue was recognition of the council, but underlying this was not only the question of images, but also relations with the other patriarchates and the question of imperial authority.

The Stephen episode reveals other aspects of Constantine V's regime. The first was the Emperor's alliance with the populace of the capital. He used the hippodrome and the races to mobilize popular support. Constantine's iconoclasm was far from being just an 'imperial heresy'. It had a popular basis, which would ensure that he was remembered with affection long after his death. The hippodrome became the venue for the ritual humiliation of opponents of the regime. The people took part with enthusiasm. There is a vivid scene from the Life of Stephen the Younger. One of the Emperor's favourites had joined Stephen and had embraced the monastic life. He had been rescued and brought back to the capital, where the Emperor displayed him in the hippodrome. His monastic habit was removed and thrown to the crowd. He was then washed clean and arrayed in a military uniform. As a final act of reconciliation, the Emperor – to the acclaim of the people – hung a sword around his shoulders. This was a ritual that opposed the army to the monastic order. It was a scene that identified the Emperor's sources of support in the people and in the army. Constantine's more brutal implementation of his iconoclast policies may owe something to the need to please his supporters.

Members of the imperial administration were always less than enthusiastic about iconoclasm. Stephen had several devotees among leading palace officials and his death at the hands of the mob was the signal for a conspiracy against the Emperor, which included those at the heart of the Byzantine establishment. It was the more dangerous for the tacit support of the patriarch Constantine. The Emperor first sent the Patriarch into exile and then brought him back to the capital, where he was paraded around the hippodrome. He was ritually humiliated before being executed, the fate of other members of the conspiracy.

The suppression of the conspiracy was accompanied by an attack on the monastic order. Hitherto Constantine V had been well disposed towards monasteries. He was a patron, for instance, of Anthousa, the founder and director of the double monastery of Mantineion, and named one of his daughters after her. Although, it is claimed, she cured him of temporary blindness, this did not prevent the Emperor later taking action against her. One of his agents is supposed to have tortured her by pouring burning icons over her. This may just be a fictitious hagiographical detail, for otherwise Constantine's actions were more prosaic. In Constantinople monks and nuns were paraded around the hippodrome and reviled by the populace. Then they were forced to abandon their monastic vows and to marry. Military governors were encouraged to treat members of monastic orders in the provinces in the same way. At the same time, monastic property was confiscated and monastic buildings were turned over to military use.

The Emperor's opponents linked this attack on monasteries with his growing hostility towards the cult of saints. He was supposed to have destroyed relics, and it was alleged that those who made offerings to the saints because of their health were 'threatened with death, confiscation, exile, or torture on the grounds of impiety'. The latter action is out of keeping with the Emperor's earlier writings, where he went out of his way to approve the intercession of the Mother of God and the saints; so out of keeping that one suspects some exaggeration on the part of hostile sources. At the bottom of Constantine's anti-monastic policy was the refusal by some monks to accept the Council of 754. Their grounds for doing so were only partly to do with icons; imperial interference in dogma was just as important. By this time monastic circles would have absorbed the teachings of John of Damascus. He singled out icons as essential to the living tradition of Christianity. It could be argued that monasticism was equally part of the same tradition and just as vulnerable to imperial pressure. As with images, monastic status had no clear biblical basis. A monk was not ordained in the way that a priest was, yet often laid claim to more extravagant spiritual powers.

The controversy over icons revealed how interconnected different aspects of Christian worship were. An attack on icons had implications for the role of the monks and, in general, for the ordering of a Christian society. Constantine did not carry out a general persecution of monks, though this is what his opponents liked to convey; there were some abbots and monasteries who cooperated with the imperial authorities. Nor is Constantine likely to have doubted the value and validity of the intercession of saints. It was much more that he wished to clamp down on the magical practices associated with the cult of saints, which often focused on icons. He objected to monks selling the services of saints, and to holy men receiving the reflected glory of the saints. There were too many charlatans. Constantine's main intention may well have been to break monastic opposition to the Council of 754, but he also wished to give clearer direction to the monastic ideal, the stress being on its utility – spiritual and charitable – to society. Monastic behaviour should conform to the iconoclast's ethical theory of images. It was part of the way Constantine was trying to reshape Christian society so that it revolved around properly constituted authority. It was an attempt to revive imperial authority as reflected in the legislation of Justinian, but tacitly abandoning the claims to universal authority. Constantine's concern was with Byzantium; his horizons scarcely extended beyond its frontiers. His was a narrow and inward-looking concept of a Christian Empire, which owed much to the Old Testament.

THE COUNCIL OF 787

When Constantine V died in 775, his achievement seemed assured, but within scarcely ten years it was to be overturned. How is this reversal to be explained? It has much to do with Constantine's daughter-in-law Irene, who was the main force behind the restoration of images. She seems always to have been a convinced devotee of icons. This was not a factor that was likely to have counted when Constantine V selected her as the bride for his son and heir, Leo IV (775–80). More important was her birthplace, Athens. This was of some strategic importance at a time when the piecemeal recovery of the Greek lands was just beginning. When Leo IV died, Irene was left as regent for her young son, Constantine VI. Opposed by her brothers-in-law and by much of the army, she looked for support from the palace and administration, where there had always been elements sympathetic to the restoration of images. Within the church the argument that Byzantium was cutting itself off from the rest of the Christian world began to weigh more heavily. The patriarch Paul (780–4) resigned on exactly these grounds and insisted that it was imperative that a full ecumenical council be held forthwith. The man chosen to succeed him, a civil servant called Tarasius, would accept the patriarchal throne only if an ecumenical council were convened and the question of icons reopened. This duly happened in 786, but the meeting was broken up by the guards regiments. Their action met with the approval of a number of the bishops.

Irene acted swiftly. She brought in troops loyal to her and disbanded the guards regiments. The site of the council was moved from the capital to Nicaea, where the council met in 787. There were representatives of the see of Rome and of the oriental patriarchates present to give it the necessary ecumenical complexion. The Council of 787 condemned the iconoclast Council of 754 but failed to deal with the iconoclast arguments, with their ethical and Christological implications. It rescinded the anathema pronounced against John of Damascus in 754, but did not cite his works among the authorities collected to support the validity of images. The fathers of the council stressed that icons were not, as iconoclasts supposed, the invention of painters, but conformed to the tradition of the church. They were a natural accompaniment to the gospel story, with the difference that the power of sight gave them greater intensity. To rebut the iconoclast charge that icons produced a confusion of worship and veneration, the council emphasized that the icon only ever received veneration. Even then, this was directed to the likeness of the figure portrayed, not to the materials of the icon, for, in the words of the fathers of the council, 'We are moved by a desire and affection to reach the originals.'

It was hoped that the Council of 787 would provide a basis for reconciliation within the church. There was no outright con-demnation of the emperors Leo III and Constantine V. Bishop Constantine of Nakoleia, long since dead, was blamed as the true originator of iconoclasm. Taking part in the Second Council of Nicaea (usually referred to as Second Nicaea) were seventeen bishops who had participated in the Council of 754. Their fate was an important consideration that exercised the large monastic represen-tation at the council – just under a third of those present were monks. The monks were opposed to the reintegration of the majority of iconoclast bishops. One point at issue was whether any of the bishops had been forced to become iconoclasts. Hypatius of Nicaea admitted that in his case no coercion was required; he had grown up with iconoclasm. The force of his admission hit the other bishops. They agreed with him and exclaimed, 'We have all sinned, we all ask for pardon.' Despite the reservations of the monks, the iconoclast bishops were readmitted to the church under pressure from the patriarch Tarasius (784–806). One monastic leader, Sabas of Stoudios, hinted that the Patriarch was just carrying out instructions from the Empress; in other words, he was not to be trusted to uphold the independence of the church.

The monks were an uncomfortable presence at Second Nicaea. Still more worrying were those monks who had refused to attend the council on the grounds that the bishops were simonaic, while lurking in the background were those monks who had compromised with the iconoclasts. Constantine V's persecution had revealed the divisions among the monastic order, which continued after Second Nicaea and had the effect of radicalizing the monastic agenda. There was a deep suspicion of Tarasius and of his successor as patriarch, Nicephorus (806–15). Both were originally civil servants who were imposed at the head of the church of Constantinople. Standing for cooperation and compromise, they worked for reconciliation and approved as unobjectionable the cult of the cross, which had been central to iconoclasm. Elements among the monastic order thought that Tarasius and Nicephorus were too lenient on iconoclasm and too willing to compromise with imperial demands.

Equally, they subscribed to another iconoclast notion: the ethical theory of images. The great exemplar was St Philaretos the Merciful, a charitably minded Paphlagonian landowner. His Christian high-mindedness and his devotion to charity reduced him to poverty, from which he was rescued when one of his daughters was chosen to be the bride of Constantine VI (780–97). Relocated in the capital, Philaretos continued his charitable pursuits; indeed, nobody better exemplifies the iconoclast ethic of the pious layman devoted to good works. His activities aroused the suspicions of the more radical of the monks, who deliberately replaced his incipient cult in the capital with that of a fictitious martyr for images.

At this juncture a new monastic leader began to make his mark. His name was Theodore. He came from an administrative family and was the nephew of one of the leading abbots who attended

Second Nicaea. In 794 he became abbot of the Constantinopolitan monastery of Stoudios, perhaps the most powerful and respected of the capital's monasteries. His first test came when Constantine VI decided to put aside his first wife, Philaretos's daughter, and marry her lady-in-waiting, who happened to be one of Theodore's cousins. This was a scandal: the first time that a Christian emperor had divorced his empress. There was opposition, but Patriarch Tarasius tamely acceded in the face of the Emperor's threat to restore iconoclasm. Theodore was shocked by the Patriarch's pusillanimity and created a schism within the church. For his pains, he was sent into exile, but not for long, because the Emperor was himself deposed within a few months. Theodore nevertheless refused to let the matter drop and revived the schism under the next patriarch, Nicephorus. Once again he was sent into exile.

SECOND ICONOCLASM

Theodore would be recalled in the aftermath of one of the many military disasters that punctuate Byzantine history. In 811 the emperor, also called Nicephorus (802–11), was caught with his army by the Bulgarians in the Balkan passes. He was killed and his army routed. The Bulgarian chieftain, Khan Krum, advanced on Constantinople. The new emperor, Nicephorus's son-in-law, put his trust in the monks led by Theodore of Stoudios. This did not seem to be the best way of confronting a military emergency. Popular and military elements within the capital revived the memory of Constantine V. Iconoclast sympathizers prised open the entrance to the imperial tombs at the Church of the Holy Apostles and worshipped at his tomb. The story was put around that Constantine V had been seen leaving his tomb and leading the defence of the city against the Bulgars. This was the prelude to an iconoclast coup that had many of the marks of a popular uprising and brought an army commander called Leo to the throne in 813. Once Leo had dealt with the Bulgar threat, he turned to the question of images. Patriarch Nicephorus did not prove amenable to pressure and was deposed in 815, shortly before a Council of the Church assembled and restored iconoclasm in conformity with the Council of 754. Leo V (813–20) appointed a new iconoclast patriarch, Theodotos (815–21).

The restoration of iconoclasm built on the popular base created by Constantine V. It seems to have been generally welcome. There was little in the way of persecution. All that the new regime asked for was communion with the new patriarch. Most bishops and abbots were willing to comply, leaving the ex-patriarch, Nicephorus, and Theodore of Stoudios isolated. The iconoclasts made little or no effort to develop the arguments of Constantine V. These seemed more than adequate and received additional support from the iconoclast *florilegium*, or anthology, compiled by John the Grammarian, who provided much of the intellectual weight behind the new phase of iconoclasm. John's interests spread far beyond theology and revealed how a controversy over images touched on much larger intellectual issues. One of the charges levelled against Constantine V by his opponents had been the secularization of art and culture. As a result of Constantine's enthusiasm for the hippodrome, racing scenes and charioteers had been reintroduced into the repertoire of imperial art. It seems not to have gone much further than this, but it did point to a real problem, which the iconoclasts identified: the tendency for the distinction between sacred and profane to become increasingly blurred as the sacred began to invade all areas of life and culture. Iconoclasm now tried to re-establish clear boundaries.

A victim of this tendency to muddle sacred and profane was the independent study of secular, or classical, learning. Education to any level was largely confined to a few leading families in the capital. The early education of Theodore of Stoudios and his brother, for example, had been at the hands of their mother and, later, their uncle, a civil servant. Then, suddenly, in the late eighth century the standard of education improved remarkably. There was also a much wider demand, as is evident from the grammar book of George of Choiroboskos, which came out in the late eighth century and presented the grammatical treatises of late antiquity in an accessible form. George was the archivist of St Sophia, but his religious affiliations are not clear. A contemporary of his among the patriarchal clergy was Ignatios the Deacon, who was to become iconoclast bishop of Nicaea. Ignatios claimed that he had rescued classical learning, and the elegance of his letters shows that this was no idle boast.

The second phase of iconoclasm was the beneficiary of this improved standard of education. Its most significant intellectual figure was Leo the Mathematician, a cousin of John the Grammarian and, briefly, iconoclast bishop of Thessaloniki (840–43). Born and educated at Constantinople, Leo is said to have acquired his impressive scientific and mathematical knowledge on the island of Andros. It is just conceivable that as a well-connected young man he had been sent from the capital to Greece to search out manuscripts in remote monasteries, but that is all. Leo's reputation as a scholar was soon such that the caliph Ma'mun (813–33) invited him to Baghdad, where there was a revival of classical science. Leo was thoroughly acquainted with the scientific, mathematical, and astronomical texts of antiquity. A marginal note that he contributed to a manuscript of Euclid's *Elements* has survived. He also possessed a manuscript of Ptolemy's *Syntaxis*, his great work on astronomy, better known in the West as the *Almagest*. The famous illustrated Vatican Ptolemy is evidence of this revival of interest in Greek science, but though it can be dated to the early 830s, it did not, so it seems, belong to Leo. It is still a work of immense accomplishment and was most likely intended as an official gift.

The surprising number of scientific manuscripts that survive from the second period of iconoclasm are testimony to the revival of secular learning, which reached its culmination in the reign of Theophilos (829–42). Despite his iconoclasm, Theophilos was remembered as a good ruler with a zeal for justice. He was also a great builder. He made additions to the imperial palace, which impressed contemporaries with their lavish use of marble and precious metals. He had automata – such as mechanical birds singing from gilded boughs – constructed for the throne room in emulation of the Abbasid court, just as his suburban palace of Bryas was constructed along the lines of an Abbasid pleasure dome.

This vogue for Abbasid style fits with the secularization of the court of Theophilos, but was paradoxical in that this emperor had to face the last serious Arab assault on Byzantium. In 838 Caliph Mut'asim (833–42) defeated Theophilos and then captured Amorion, the capital of the Anatolic theme and the birthplace of the Emperor's father. It was a terrible blow to the dynasty's prestige and was seen as a judgement on its iconoclasm. This was the theme of the *Forty-Two Martyrs of Amorion*, an acount of soldiers led away into captivity from the sack of the town, who refused to apostasize to Islam and were executed. The defeats of 838 prepared the way for the liquidation of iconoclasm after Theophilos's death in 842.

TRIUMPH OF ORTHODOXY

During the second period of iconoclasm the emperors had had little difficulty in dealing with opposition. The main opponents were Patriarch Nicephorus, who died in 828, and Theodore of Stoudios, who died in 826. They were old enemies and there was little love lost between them. The deposed Patriarch behaved very properly. He made no attempt at direct interference in ecclesiastical matters, but spent his retirement working on a rebuttal of iconoclast theology, which made little impact at the time. Theodore of Stoudios did not submit with the equanimity that the Patriarch showed. He became the centre of outright opposition to iconoclasm. By dint of a vast correspondence he maintained a circle of supporters, some of whom had influence at court. After years of exile he was allowed to spend his last years in comfortable retirement.

Though less than heroic, Nicephorus and Theodore of Stoudios did much to prepare the way for the restoration of images. They provided a defence of images that took into account the higher level of intellectual attainment that now existed among the Byzantine elite. Their arguments owed much to Aristotelian logic (even if they presented them as based on 'the power of the truth'), which gave them the intellectual armoury to face up to Constantine V's iconoclast theology. They were able to dispose of his famous argument about the consequences of circumscribing Christ: that is, you *either* confused *or* separated his natures. Theodore and Nicephorus saw that the iconoclasts assumed that the process of circumscribing Christ was the work of an artist. But, they objected, this was not it at all: the process was instead the inevitable consequence of the miracle of the Incarnation. It was for exactly this reason that images bore witness to the Incarnation. As such, they conformed to the teaching of the Council of Chalcedon, which insisted on Christ having two perfect natures, human and divine, united without confusion or division. The iconoclast refusal to depict Christ was a denial of the Incarnation: that Christ was both man and God.

Nicephorus and Theodore of Stoudios took issue with Constantine V's assertion that image and prototype must possess an essential identity. It was this that underpinned the iconoclasts' insistence that the Eucharist was the true image of Christ, always one of their most powerful arguments. Nicephorus and Theodore turned it on its head by suggesting that by treating the Eucharist as merely an image of Christ the iconoclasts were impugning the real presence. The latter's definition was, in any case, impracticably restrictive. The two iconodule leaders argued instead for a relative identity, which meant that an image would enjoy relative participation in the honours and the virtues of the original. In that way the ethical theory of images, which the iconodules did not dispute, could be applied to the images themselves. Just as the virtuous Christian participated, however remotely, in the qualities of Christ and his saints, so an image could. It was a well-argued but less restrictive view of the role of images, which at the same time guarded against the worst excesses of icon veneration.

Theodore of Stoudios had done his work very well in another way too. After his death his network of supporters continued the tradition of resistance. Stoudios monastery was a focus for discontented elements in the church and at court. It was irritating enough for Emperor Theophilos to renew persecution. The painter Lazaros had his hands cauterized on the Emperor's orders, but this did not prevent him from returning to the painting of icons the moment he was released. Other victims were the Graptoi (literally, 'inscribed') brothers, so called because they had iambic verses tattooed across their foreheads identifying them as 'foul vessels of perverted heresy'.

More dangerous was the patrician Sergios, who was exiled in 832 for his iconophile beliefs. He was the father of the future patriarch Photius; his wife was a relative by marriage of Theophilos's empress, Theodora. He was, in other words, at the heart of Byzantine political life. Just as there had been civil servants who were opposed to Constantine V over images, so there were under Theophilos. The reason for this is likely to have had something to do with the politics of the court. Civil servants may have felt at a disadvantage under iconoclast regimes, which tended to be militaristic. They may also have objected to the lengths that Constantine V and Theophilos went to court popular support. Their opposition must also have been connected with fashions in piety. Civil servants were the best educated group within the empire, so they could appreciate the debate over images better than others. It was clear that the intellectual case for images had prevailed, thanks to the elaboration of John of Damascus's ideas by Nicephorus and Theodore.

In the end, the restoration of images in 843 was an inside job, the work of Empress Theodora, supported by her closest relatives. Theodora simply reinstated Second Nicaea and marked the occasion, known as the Triumph of Orthodoxy, with a new festival, the Feast of Orthodoxy, designed to celebrate annually the triumph over heresy. Because the restoration of images was on both occasions the work of empresses supported by their cliques of relatives and sympathizers, many historians have assumed that there was a natural empathy between women and icons. There was even a presumption that women responded more readily to the magical and emotional aspects of Christian worship. There are charming stories of the empresses Irene and Theodora keeping icons in their private apartments. Other women of the imperial family are equally supposed to have been secret devotees of icons. That this was generally true of women from the leading court families is suggested by the fact that forty women were numbered among Theodore of Stoudios's active correspondents. At a different level of society, the wife of St Stephen the Younger's jailer kept icons hidden from her husband, which she allowed the saint to venerate. Women as well as men may have taken part in Stephen's death on the streets of the capital, but it remains the case that icons had long been the focus of household devotions, which were the special concern of the women of the family. There are enough examples to show how powerful women were within the bosom of the family and how they determined the religious tenor of family life. Since it was public conformity that iconoclast emperors were most anxious to secure, it is more than possible that women were left to carry on domestic devotions undisturbed.

Underlying the iconoclast controversy was a struggle for the whole character of Byzantine civilization, which was played out in many petty dramas that elude us. But the main issues are clear. The cult of images developed over the sixth and seventh centuries with little or no scrutiny, and threatened to monopolize Christian worship. Critics who saw this as little different from idolatry had a point, as images assumed magical or talismanic properties and laid

Byzantium open to criticism from Jews and Muslims. Reliance on images transformed Christian worship and blurred all kinds of boundaries. It threatened that sense of hierarchy that underlay the proper order of Byzantine society. It demanded a clear definition of the role and function of images. In the end this was what the iconoclast controversy provided, the opponents of images contributing at least as much as their defenders. Before the outbreak of iconoclasm, miracle-working images featured prominently. At Second Nicaea the fathers had drawn up a catalogue of wonder-working images, but after the definitive restoration of images in 843 iconophiles preferred to draw a veil over their magical properties. Their achievement was to safeguard the role of religious art as a necessary accompaniment of the liturgy and as an aid to contemplation. This gave Byzantine civilization a clear imprint that distinguished it from Latin Christendom and even more from Islam. Iconoclasm was sterile in religious terms. It was too literal and failed to recognize that all religious systems have to have the capacity to develop to meet new eventualities. It is easy now to criticize iconodule thinkers, such as John of Damascus, for fabricating evidence in order to provide icons with the necessary New Testament and patristic authority. But their emphasis on a continuing tradition that was capable of incorporating new elements was of a piece with their conviction that the miracle of the Incarnation continued to work – it was the essence of Christ's legacy, passed on by apostles and saints.

In the short term iconoclasm was of immense benefit to Byzantium. Leo III and Constantine V used it as a cover for the restoration of the bases of imperial authority, which had been compromised by the triumph of Islam. This allowed Byzantium to escape from the political anarchy into which it had descended in the first decades of the eighth century. The iconoclast emperors passed on effective imperial authority, which underpinned the achievements of the Macedonian dynasty in the late ninth and tenth centuries. Iconoclasm also challenged the monastic domination of culture, which had been a feature of the seventh century. The level of education rose; secular learning was cultivated for its own sake and there was a recovery of many aspects of classical culture. It restored to Byzantine culture a balance that was being lost.

Chapter Six

BYZANTIUM AND THE WEST

I t was in the course of the iconoclast dispute that Western Christendom emerged as a distinct entity, its ties to Constantinople and Eastern Christendom more or less severed. Charlemagne's imperial coronation in Rome on Christmas Day 800 has long been taken as the symbolic event marking this separation, but the unity of the two halves of the Roman Empire was always artificial. However much cross-fertilization there may have been over the centuries, however common bilingualism may have been among the educated elite, there always remained two distinct cultures: one Latin and the other Greek. This was disguised by the triumph of Christianity and by the shift of the imperial capital to Constantinople. The West – and this included the Barbarian successor kingdoms – looked to the emperor at Constantinople as the ultimate arbiter. One of the effects of transferring the capital to Constantinople was that Latin became the language of the army and the administration in the East, even if Greek remained the language of the church and culture. It was a development that went some way towards softening the divide between the East and the West.

THE TIES WEAKEN

It was in this environment that the great Latin theologian Augustine was able to assimilate new ideas emanating from the Cappadocian fathers in the East. However, these ideas were fed into a distinctively Western theological outlook, which Augustine did more than anybody else to create. He ensured that its concerns and characteristics were very different from those of the East. Its emphasis was on predestination and community, not on intercession and perfectibility. Though new currents of thought continued to seep in from the East, they were subjected to careful scrutiny on the basis of Augustine's theology. In this process of conceptual and cultural exchange that went on during the early Middle Ages the West may have been the junior partner, but it was far from passive. It was a process that was possible because a sense of unity based on a shared faith and common political loyalties lasted into the eighth century and was cemented at the level of the elite by personal ties. Pope Gregory the Great (590–604) belonged to the Anicius family, which a century before had produced Juliana Anicia, a benefactress of Constantinople. Gregory himself had been papal 'nuncio' (*apocrisarius*) at Constantinople before becoming pope.

Such ties were reinforced by Justinian's reconquest of Italy, Sicily, and North Africa, and, if anything, strengthened by the Lombard invasions, which sent Roman senators scurrying for the safety of Constantinople. Cassiodorus was an exception. He stayed on at Vivarium, the monastery he had founded in southern Italy. Here he was able to complete the work of his older contemporary Boethius, whose project it was to make 'Greek wisdom' available to the Latin West. While Boethius translated and commented upon Aristotle's logic, Cassiodorus produced the *Institutes*, a textbook that presented the classical curriculum in a Christian form. The slightly later compilation by Isidore, Bishop of Seville, known as the *Etymologies*, does much the same in a Spanish context. The work of these men was important for the revival of learning in the Carolingian period. In a somewhat basic form they were able to preserve for the Latin West the fundamentals of Greek education and learning as they existed in the Justinianic era.

Far from undermining the close ties of Byzantium and Rome, the Monothelete controversy of the seventh century testified to a working relationship. Dissidents in Constantinople looked to Rome for refuge and support. In the end, the Roman position triumphed. The links uniting Constantinople and Rome solidified as more and more refugees from the East settled in Rome in the wake of the Arab conquests. There was a series of popes for whom Greek was the first language. For a time Greek threatened to become the language of the curia. For example, when Wilfred, Bishop of York, went to Rome at the beginning of the eighth century to petition the papacy, the papal synod discussed his case in Greek. The number of Greek-speaking monasteries in Rome grew, and it was from these that the popes of the seventh and eighth centuries drew many of their experts. Theodore of Tarsus, dispatched as Archbishop of Canterbury in the mid-seventh century, is the best example.

On the eve of iconoclasm Rome was still a great city by the standards of the day, much reduced as it might have been since its imperial heyday. There were imposing pilgrimage churches, such as St Peter's, that went back to the time of Constantine. There was a series of fifth-century basilicas built by the popes of the time. Some great classical buildings survived, such as the Castel San Angelo, as it was known to the Middle Ages, or the Pantheon, which was converted into the Church of Santa Maria Rotonda in 609. A little earlier a first-century audience hall was transformed into the Church of Santa Maria Antiqua. At the beginning of the eighth century Pope John VII (705–7) had it decorated with a series of highly accomplished frescoes. Whether the artists came from Constantinople or not is less important than the fact that these frescoes demonstrate that Rome and Constantinople belonged to the same world. Pope John was himself the son of a Byzantine official. Although he may have been at loggerheads with Justinian II over recognition of the canons of the Council in Troullo, in 711 his successor but one as pope dutifully made his way to Constantinople, where he was received with honour, and yet again there was some kind of reconciliation between Constantinople and Rome.

This working relationship was compromised by the actions of Emperor Leo III. It started when, in 724 or 725, he imposed taxation on the papal patrimonies in southern Italy and Sicily, which had previously been exempted. It was compounded by his 'iconoclast' decree of 730, to which both Pope Gregory II and his successor, Pope Gregory III, were bitterly opposed. In the first place, so much of the ecclesiastical history of the past two and a half centuries had been, at least on the surface, a matter of Rome showing Constantinople where orthodoxy lay. In the second, icons were an integral part of Rome's religious life, just as they had become in any other Byzantine city. Icons were used in processions; the icon of Christ of the Lateran became the palladium of the city and it was believed to be a miraculous image, not made by human hand. Icons were used to promote cults at Rome. Thus while the cult of the Mother of God at Constantinople centred on relics, such as the girdle and the veil, at Rome it was on images. The cult of the Mother of God is a good example of a Byzantine import into the religious life of Rome. When in 609 the Pantheon was converted into a church in her honour, an icon of Mary was sent from Constantinople to mark the occasion. Pope Sergius I (687–701) ordered that her feast days of the Nativity, Annunciation, and Assumption be celebrated officially by processions. John VII was another devotee. The icon known as the Madonna della Clemenza shows him kissing Mary's foot. Appropriately, in an iconography that originated in Rome, Mary is shown arrayed like an empress, as she is in a mosaic – originally in St Peter's – also commissioned by John VII in which he approaches her, proclaiming himself to be 'the

Servant of the Holy Mother of God'. The Pope was using the cult for political ends. While Justinian II had appropriated the title 'Servant of God', John VII emphasized the papacy's exalted position within the Byzantine hierarchy through the cult of the Mother of God. Christ and his mother were the focus of much Christian piety. At Rome this was given special emphasis by a custom that was developing for the Feast of the Assumption. The icon of the Christ of the Lateran would be taken in procession to Santa Maria Maggiore to visit the icon of the Mother of God housed there, popularly believed to be a work of St Luke.

Leo III's 'iconoclast' decree gave deep offence to Roman piety. It was also a threat to papal prestige in that it challenged Pope Gregory the Great's pronouncement on the validity of religious art, which was contained in two letters that he wrote to Serenus, Bishop of Marseilles, in 599 and 600. It is one of the most important statements about the function of religious art in a Christian context, if only because it became the foundation of Western views on art in the Middle Ages. Gregory's letters were used and reinterpreted over and over again. The Pope had heard that the Bishop of Marseilles was destroying religious paintings in his diocese on the grounds that there were those among his flock who were adoring them in a way that should have been reserved for the Trinity alone. Gregory allowed that, if this was the case, it was reprehensible and had to be repressed, but thought that the Bishop had shown excessive zeal. Religious pictures had a legitimate place in Christian worship. The Pope told Serenus that 'pictures are displayed in churches on this account, so that those who are illiterate may at least read by seeing on the walls what they are unable to read in books'. Gregory was developing the theme of religious art as the 'books of the illiterate'. He was not concerned with icons as such in his letters to Serenus – his discussion centred on the narrative scenes decorating churches – but his views would be applied to religious art generally. Gregory was clear that images were not to be worshipped, but he had nothing specific to say about whether they might receive lesser forms of honour, and the large number of votive images intruded into the main decoration of Roman churches at this time reveals a veneration of images of the kind that had developed in Byzantium.

Rome's reaction to the iconoclast controversy followed a time-honoured pattern. In 731 Pope Gregory III called a synod to protest at and condemn the innovations imposed unilaterally by the Byzantine emperor. Opponents of iconoclasm fled Byzantium for the safety of Rome. This was symbolized in the story of the icon known as Santa Maria Romana, which, at Patriarch Germanos I's bidding, swam all the way to Rome and all the way back again once iconoclasm was over! The Byzantine refugees strengthened Greek monasticism, which became an important component of Roman life. In the eighth century perhaps a quarter of Rome's monasteries were Greek, and this persisted into the ninth century. During the second phase of iconoclasm supporters of images looked to Rome for support. Theodore of Stoudios believed that the papacy had the right to condemn an illegal synod. He claimed that in such circumstances 'the bishop of Rome is accorded the power of the ecumenical council'. Only the pope, in Theodore's opinion, had the authority to settle the schism within the church of Constantinople, which the renewal of iconoclasm had produced. Pope Paschal I (817–24) installed Greek monks when he founded San Prassede, to which he attached the Zeno chapel as a funerary monument for his mother. The iconography of this chapel has been singled out for its Byzantine spirit. It is neither didactic nor decorative, but was designed to make a series of dogmatic statements. The chapel contains premonitions of the way in which Byzantine church decoration would develop in the course of the late ninth and tenth centuries.

THE PAPACY'S BALANCING ACT

We can see that old patterns of opposition and empathy persisted, and this despite radical transformations that occurred in Italy in the middle years of the eighth century. In 731 Ravenna, the Byzantine capital in Italy, fell to the Lombards. Thanks to papal initiative, the Lombards returned Ravenna in 743. It is not clear, however, whether the Pope was acting for the good of Byzantium or on his own account. In any case, the restoration was of short duration. In 751 Ravenna was reclaimed by the Lombards. With the Byzantine hold on Ravenna relaxed, the papacy had to fend for itself. It negotiated with the Lombards on behalf of the 'holy republic and the Christ-loved Roman army'. The idea that papal Rome constituted an independent political unit was starting to take shape. But the shadow of Byzantium was still there. The Lateran Palace was remodelled at this time on lines suggested by the imperial palace at Constantinople. Pope Zacharias (741–52) added a Chalke Gate as the ceremonial entrance into the papal palace, and Pope Leo III (795–816) added a Chrysotriklinos as the main reception and banqueting hall.

Despite these pretensions, the papacy needed a protector against the Lombards. Pope Stephen III (752–57) hurried across the Alps in the late autumn of 753 to seek the support of Pepin, the ruler of the Franks. Their meeting at Ponthieu in January 754 was decisive. The Pope anointed Pepin king of the Franks. In return, Pepin promised to recover Ravenna for the papacy. In 756 a charter, the so-called 'Donation of Pepin', confirmed that the old exarchate of Ravenna now constituted a papal territory. The papacy had obtained what it wanted, while the Franks began to weigh up an entanglement that was likely to have complications. They had hitherto been blithely indifferent to the question of images, but their involvement in Italy made them aware of a serious difference separating the papacy from the Byzantine church. In 767 there was a conference at Gentilly, which took place under Frankish auspices. Its purpose was mainly diplomatic: to resolve the Italian situation. Present were delegations from Rome and Constantinople. Pepin wanted the theological differences separating the papacy and Byzantium, including the question of images, debated. This demonstrated an awareness on the part of the Frankish ruler that his involvement with the papacy had a theological dimension; that the interests of the Frankish church were not necessarily the same as those of the papacy; and that he had the power to make the papacy explain itself.

The papacy had a certain amount of explaining to do. An aristocratic faction had foisted one of their number, named Constantine, on the throne of St Peter. A council was called in 769 to deal with the matter. Frankish bishops were specifically invited, another indication of how much the papacy needed the Franks to regulate its affairs. The council concentrated on the scandal and affirmed that the election of a pope was henceforth to be the prerogative of the Roman clergy and the new pope was then to be acclaimed by the militia and people of Rome. The council also formally condemned the iconoclast Council of 754. It was a means of emphasizing that Rome was no longer under Byzantine tutelage.

After the turmoil of the preceding years the election of Hadrian in 772 ushered in a period of stability in Rome. Hadrian came from the inner circle of the Roman clergy, rather than from one of the aristocratic factions. His uncle and guardian was Theodotus, a papal functionary, whose donor portraits are still to be seen in the Church of Santa Maria Antiqua. Theodotus was the administrator of the *diaconia* attached to the church. *Diaconiae* were welfare organizations run under the auspices of the papacy. Hadrian brought this tradition of good works to his papacy and set about restoring the city of Rome. He repaired the Aurelian walls and the aqueducts, and refurbished many of the ancient churches. Of greater practical importance was his reorganization of papal estates around Rome. Their increased revenues went to the *diaconiae* of the city to meet welfare needs within the city. It was the most effective way of reasserting papal dominance of Rome.

Hadrian's accession to the throne of St Peter coincided with direct Frankish intervention against the Lombards. In 774 Charlemagne annexed the Lombard kingdom of Pavia. In the midst of his siege of Pavia he decided that he wished to spend Easter at Rome. He was welcomed as Patrician of the Romans. He first made his way to St Peter's to pray at the apostle's tomb, which was outside the city walls. Charlemagne then observed protocol by seeking permission from the pope to enter the city. In some ways the end of the Lombard kingdom benefited the papacy: there was greater security and there was a greater opportunity to create a papal state in central Italy out of the former exarchate of Ravenna. The disadvantage was that the papacy faced much closer supervision from the Franks. Though there will always be uncertainties about the Donation of Constantine – the most famous forgery of the Middle Ages – it was at this time that the charter was taking shape. Its purpose was to strengthen the papacy's hand in its dealings with the Franks. The story was that, when Constantine transferred his capital from Rome to Constantinople, he granted Pope Sylvester imperial prerogatives in the West. The legend took clearer shape in the course of the eighth century as the papacy was forced to defend its independence in the face of Byzantine, Lombard, and, finally, Frankish claims.

Hadrian I will have been gratified by the feelers put out by Empress Irene for a papal presence at a council to restore the veneration of images. Her action was clear recognition of what Rome saw as its traditional role: the preservation of the faith. Just as so often in the past, its stand was about to be vindicated. Irene's invitation also emphasized the papacy's independent status at a time when it seemed half in tutelage to the Franks. Hadrian was far too aware of protocol not to include the name of Charlemagne in his correspondence with the Byzantine court. The fact that the Byzantines chose to excise it from their version of the correspondence was to have unfortunate consequences, since it led to a distinct coolness between Charlemagne and the papacy over the question of images. While Charlemagne broke off diplomatic relations with Byzantium, Pope Hadrian persevered. There were two papal legates, both appropriately called Peter, present when the council finally assembled at Nicaea in September 787. Their position as representatives of the senior see in Christendom was respected: they head the list of those who put their signature to the acts of the council, and both signed on behalf of Pope Hadrian. The council was, however, only a limited success for the papacy. The papal legates did not feature prominently in the debates. Nor were they able to have the Roman 'proof texts', which included Gregory the Great's letter to Serenus, entered into the official record of the council. Iconoclasm was not categorically condemned as a heresy, as Hadrian had wished. His letter to the council was doctored to suit the Byzantines. His emphasis on the primacy of Rome was ignored and the papacy was treated as part of the pentarchy of patriarchates. Hadrian had praised Charlemagne and offered him as a model Christian ruler whose example the Byzantines would do well to follow, but this section of the letter was not read out to the council. The council was deaf to Hadrian's request for the return of the papal patrimonies together with ecclesiastical jurisdiction over southern Italy, Sicily, and Illyricum.

Despite these setbacks Rome's position as the upholder of orthodox belief was clearly accepted by Byzantium. The council could therefore be presented as a triumph for the papacy. Hadrian never condemned it and, in the face of growing Frankish disquiet about the proceedings, stubbornly defended its validity, despite the appalling translation of the acts of the council from Greek into Latin, for which he has to take ultimate responsibility. The translation made a mockery of the careful formulations of the council. The Greek theologians made sure that they maintained a clear distinction between *latreia* (divine adoration and worship), which belonged to the Trinity alone, and *proskynesis* (honorific veneration), which was appropriate to images as well as to other sacred objects and holy personages. The Latin translation used *adorare* (adoration and veneration) indiscriminately for both. Hadrian I forwarded this translation to the Frankish court because he wished to have the support of the Frankish ruler and church before he officially approved the acts of the council. The sloppiness of the translation may be a sign that he took it for granted.

THE CAROLINE BOOKS

Charlemagne's theologians were outraged by what they read. The Council of 787 appeared to be recommending idolatry, which, at a time when the Frankish armies were trying to wean the Saxons away from their idols, was inconvenient. The offending passages in the acts of the council were noted and objections to them tabled. There was a political undercurrent evident from the criticism that it was inappropriate for a woman – Empress Irene – to preside over a Church Council, but the main thrust of the objections was directed against the assumption that there was a scriptural foundation to the worship of images. The Carolingian theologians were adamant that the Bible gave no support for this practice; the reverse, in fact. Nor were they willing to accept the string of 'proof texts' adduced by the council, on the grounds that they were specious. The document, known as the *Capitulare versus synodum*, was then dispatched to Hadrian I, who set about preparing a reply that might undo some of the damage caused by the translation. He was, this time, careful to make a distinction between *adorare* and *venerare*. Hadrian singled out the Roman tradition of venerating images, which was founded on the work of Gregory the Great. He noted that both Pope Gregory III (731) and Pope Stephen III (769) had held Councils that had upheld the legitimacy of images and, more to the point, that the

Frankish church had been represented at the Council of 769 and had approved its decisions.

The papal reaction was unwelcome. It revealed a deep division of opinion about a question that Charlemagne took very seriously. His reasons for doing so are now very largely a matter of guesswork, but there was definitely a political dimension. Charlemagne felt that he had been snubbed by the Byzantines, who acted at the council as though no other Christian rulers counted. At home the continuing struggle with Germanic paganism and the vestiges of Celtic beliefs cannot be discounted. But more important was unfamiliarity with icons. This does not mean that there was no place for religious art in the Frankish church, just that its place was still very restricted. The role that images had had in Rome for two centuries or more had not spread to the rest of Western Christendom. We know that Western pilgrims and visitors to Rome brought back with them icons obtained there, but they were treated as curiosities. The focus of veneration remained the relics of saints. It seemed to Frankish churchmen that the Council of 787 was trying to raise images to the same rank as relics as objects of veneration. To accord fabrications the same honour as relics was to devalue the saints, they argued, and would produce anarchy and defections from the church. It was, above all, a challenge to the hierarchy of the church. This was something that Charlemagne understood.

With Charlemagne's encouragement, one of his leading theologians, Theodulf, Bishop of Orleans, set about producing a considered statement of the views of the Frankish church on images and related matters. His labours over the years 790–93 produced the *Libri Carolini*, or Caroline Books, the first systematic statement of a Frankish theology. However, they never had a wide circulation. They survive in one manuscript, which was prepared either for the royal or for the papal archives, where it is now to be found. Although it has long been fashionable to measure the significance of a medieval document by the number of manuscripts that have survived, this is not the only test of importance. Another is whether it reflects a particular situation or set of ideas. The Caroline Books, as we shall see, were overtaken by events, but the ideas expressed were to have a long life and to be the cause of controversy within the Frankish church for nearly a century. The Caroline Books were a prestige project. If they were mostly the work of Theodulf of Orleans, he had the support and advice of other prominent Frankish theologians, including Alcuin. When the text was completed, it was submitted to a meeting presided over by Charlemagne. A scribe noted in the margins his brief comments on the different articles. They take the form of a *bene*, an *optime*, a *perfecte*, or, even more enthusiastically, an *ecclesiastice*, which meant 'in accordance with ecclesiastical tradition'. Dismissal of the view that 'whatever Scripture treats, painters can represent' earns a *bene*, while the declaration that 'we do not therefore reject images, but only their most superstitious adoration' is greeted with a *perfecte*. The fact that it was considered worth recording Charlemagne's reactions underlines how important the work was considered at the time. Charlemagne's interest in the project is evident from the fact that a preface was supplied in his name. It was a way he could demonstrate that he was defending the church 'against the novelties of foolish synods and emperors who blasphemously claim to rule with God'.

The 'foolish synods and emperors' threatened to undermine the very foundations of the faith by raising, as it seemed to Charlemagne and his bishops, images to equal status not only with relics, but also with the scriptures and the sacraments. Such a practice flew directly in the face of the Old Testament prohibition against 'graven images'. It seemed to devalue the Old Testament, which the Franks revered for the way it prefigured the New. Therefore, any disrespect for the Old Testament threatened the validity of the New. The Frankish church clung to the primacy of the word: truth lay 'not in pictures, but in the scriptures'. This did not lead to iconoclasm, because the second commandment was balanced by Gregory's letter to Serenus, which was quoted in the Caroline Books. The most famous passage, which presents images as the 'books of the illiterate', was kept but received no particular emphasis: for the uneducated, as a matter of course, pictures took the place of scriptures. The Caroline Books preserve the thrust of Gregory's argument that it was wrong to worship images, but equally wrong to destroy them. Their function was to please the eye and to act as a memorial. The Caroline Books desacralized art; they denied any link between the representation and the original, save the name they had in common. Art was not an aid to contemplation: 'God is to be sought not in visible or fabricated things, but in the heart; He is to be gazed upon not with the eyes of the flesh, but only with the eye of the mind.' As a cautionary tale the author of the Caroline Books raises the possibility of confusing depictions of the Virgin with those of Venus. He considers that art has been irretrievably tainted by its association with classical myths and he rehearses a long series of pagan themes expressed in art. With this background it was more or less inevitable that 'false, wicked, foolish, and unsuitable' elements would be intruded into depictions of biblical narratives. It was ridiculous even to think of according images the same status as the cross or relics, let alone the Eucharist. These had all received consecration; images had not.

The worship of images offended the Frankish bishops' sense of the holy and threatened their virtual monopoly of it. The Caroline Books were very clear that the bishop was the arbiter of the holy. This claim would be impossible to enforce if images gave direct access to the divine. It would have meant cutting out the middleman: the bishop or priest. The Caroline Books sought to preserve the focus of worship on the Eucharist as a means of upholding episcopal authority. This was a reflection of the way the Frankish church remained loyal to a traditional pattern of belief, which aimed at preserving the transcendence of God. It is immediately apparent that the position of the Frankish church on images has, at first sight, much in common with that of the iconoclasts at Byzantium. But this is a superficial judgement. The circumstances of Byzantine iconoclasm were very different. Jewish and Muslim criticism of the role that images had assumed in the Byzantine church played no part in the reaction of the Frankish church. Nor was it faced with an entrenched devotion to images that was part of a deep need for individual intercessors. The reaction of the Frankish church was governed by different circumstances and considerations.

As a response to the Byzantine iconoclast controversy, the Caroline Books, it is often suggested, are irredeemably flawed because they are based on misunderstandings that result from an abysmal translation of the acts of the Council of 787. This may, in fact, have been all to the good, in that it facilitated the essential purpose of the Caroline Books, which was to work out a distinctive Frankish position on a very important question. What the Frankish theologians recognized was that the position accorded to images both at Byzantium and at Rome produced a form of worship and an understanding of the faith that were at odds with Western authorities, notably Augustine, who put more stress on community and common worship than on the need for privileged intercessors, whether they came in the form of the holy man or in the shape of the icon. Augustine had no time for religious art: he thought that 'those who have sought Christ and his apostles not in sacred books but in pictures on the wall thoroughly deserve to fall into error'. It did not surprise him in the least that such people 'are deceived, if they fashion their ideas from paintings'. Augustine placed primacy on the word of scripture. His preoccupations with sin and predestination and with the relationship of the two cities would continue to shape the concerns of the Latin church. The Caroline Books were designed to recall Latin Christianity to its basic principles in the face of Rome's flirtation with Eastern Christianity.

These principles made some impact on the art of the time. Christ in Majesty was a favourite illustration of early Carolingian gospel books, but later features less prominently in the repertoire of Carolingian art. This suggests that some religious images began to arouse scepticism. There was some agreement that the resurrected Christ was more properly contemplated in the mind's eye rather than through any artistic medium. This cast doubt on the value of images of Christ in Majesty. Old Testament themes were safer, because, like the Ark of the Covenant, they had often expressly received divine approval. They also prefigured New Testament themes. When Theodulf of Orleans built a chapel at his residence at St Germigny-des-Prés, he decorated the apse with a representation in mosaic of the Ark of the Covenant with four angels in attendance. This exemplified perfectly the teaching that he had set out in the Caroline Books.

The Caroline Books were intended as a guide for the synod that Charlemagne assembled at Frankfurt in 794 for the reformation of his kingdom and people, which coincided with a meeting of magnates that dealt with secular matters. It was only to be expected that Charlemagne would preside over the assembly of magnates, not that he would also preside over the Church Council, even taking precedence over the papal legates who were present. He was able to justify this on the grounds that 'in the stormy flux of this world the church has been committed to us for ruling'. The acts of both meetings were drawn up indiscriminately in the form of a royal capitulary. Charlemagne's domination of proceedings is apparent from the title *rector Christiani populi*, accorded to him by the assembled prelates. Charlemagne intended his synod of Frankfurt as a riposte to the Council of 787. He disputed the latter's right to call itself ecumenical. He was clear that the Frankfurt meeting was only a 'local' council, but, unlike the Second Council of Nicaea, it affirmed the traditional tenets of orthodoxy rather than introducing suspect innovations. If Byzantium was condemned, Rome and the papacy were ignored. The synod of Frankfurt proclaimed the autonomy of the Frankish church and people.

The doctrinal question considered in greatest detail at Frankfurt was the Spanish heresy of adoptionism. If less time was spent on the veneration of images, this was because the Caroline Books made long discussion unnecessary, not because Charlemagne was trying to mollify the papacy. Second Nicaea was condemned on the basis of the Caroline Books. This condemnation generated immense ill-feeling in Rome, as was evident from the way huge icons were then set up in the main places of pilgrimage. Relations between Charlemagne and Hadrian I remained cool until the latter's death a year later, on Christmas Day 795. Charlemagne tried to repair some of the damage by commissioning a suitable epitaph for Hadrian from Alcuin and having it engraved on a piece of black marble in impressively classical lettering.

THE FRANKISH EMPIRE

Hadrian I had dominated Rome. His successor, Leo III (795–816), had none of his credentials and was soon at loggerheads with the great Roman families, who chased him from the city after subjecting him to some form of blinding. Leo III needed Carolingian protection not from the Byzantines or the Lombards but from the Roman aristocracy. He understood at first hand the disadvantages of the papacy's estrangement from the Frankish ruler. Charlemagne saw it as his duty to intervene in Rome: order had to be restored. He arrived in November 800 in order to investigate the charges made against the Pope and the latter's countercharges. At some point he agreed to be crowned and anointed Roman emperor. Charlemagne's biographer, Einhard, claims that the Emperor told him that if he knew beforehand what the Pope intended, he would never have gone to Rome. This has given rise to the belief that Charlemagne was ambushed into becoming emperor. It is much more likely that Charlemagne was grumbling to the young Einhard about all the unexpected complications that his elevation to the imperial dignity produced. It is naive to think that the imperial acclamations Charlemagne received when he was making his entry into Rome on 24 November were unpremeditated. They suggest that a deal had already been struck. The papal view of the matter was set out in a mosaic that Leo III had added to his banqueting hall in the previous year. It showed St Peter handing the pallium to Leo III and a banner to Charlemagne – still entitled *king* of the Franks. This complemented a scene showing Christ handing the pallium to Pope Sylvester and the labarum to Constantine. The message was clear: Charlemagne was the new Constantine. Raising Charlemagne to the imperial dignity was a recognition of this fact, for he had already been acting out the role. At Frankfurt he had presided over a Church Council in a way reminiscent of a Constantine. His religious adviser, Alcuin, was beginning to identify the Frankish realm as a Christian empire. But Frankfurt had also pointed to a growing distance between the papacy and the Frankish ruler. Both sides were looking for reconciliation. Leo III gambled that if the Frankish ruler could be persuaded to assume the imperial title, this would have the effect of tying him more closely to Rome. It would be a way of integrating the political and ecclesiastical structures of the West and a fitting accolade of Frankish military power and Christian orthodoxy.

It might have seemed to Charlemagne a good idea at the time, but there were complications. Did the assumption of the imperial dignity alter Charlemagne's relations with his own people? Would the Franks remain loyal to him now that he was a Roman emperor? In 802 he extracted an oath of fidelity from the Franks in his new capacity. More worrying was the possibility that his imperial coronation had diminished his authority in relation to the papacy. It began to dawn on Charlemagne that his imperial coronation may not have been quite the triumphant affirmation of the power of the Frankish ruler that he at first assumed it to be, if it were interpreted in the light of the Donation of Constantine or even of Ambrose reprimanding Emperor Theodosius I. Their lesson was that the papacy had a right to supervise an emperor's moral conduct.

A further complication concerned relations with the Byzantine Empire. Did Charlemagne's imperial coronation imply a claim to the whole empire, including Byzantium? At the moment of his coronation the Byzantine Empire was in the anomalous position of being ruled over by a woman, Empress Irene, who in 797 had deposed and blinded her son, Constantine VI, the rightful emperor. Irene recognized the constitutional difficulty of her position by signing herself *basileus*, or emperor. Charlemagne offered a way out of an embarrassing position by proposing marriage to Irene, who was inclined to accept. This produced indignation at the Byzantine court and Irene's prompt overthrow in 802. Byzantine opinion was further outraged by the Frankish ruler's presumption in styling himself Roman emperor: the Byzantines were the true Romans.

A settlement was reached only in 813, when the Byzantine Empire was preoccupied with the threat from the Bulgarians. The Byzantine emperor was recognized as emperor of the Romans, while Charlemagne retained the imperial dignity in conjunction with the royal office. He signed himself 'by the grace of God emperor and augustus; and also king of the Franks and Lombards'. The claim to be Roman emperor was tacitly dropped. It suited Charlemagne rather well. He himself had crowned his son and heir, Louis the Pious, emperor without any recourse to the papacy or Rome. There were now two empires: a Frankish and a Byzantine, united ideally in fraternal love.

It was reminiscent of the late Roman Empire, when the empire had most often been divided into an eastern and a western half. If this was a parallel that diplomats on both sides will have had in mind, in retrospect we can see that it symbolized the creation of a new order, which had been emerging over the previous century. Byzantium might cling to its imperial claims, but it was no longer strictly speaking an empire, exercising universal authority. It had to recognize not just the autonomy of Western Christendom, with its distinctive Christian culture, but also a near equality of status.

THE CAROLINGIAN RENAISSANCE

Charlemagne's reign saw a blossoming of artistic and scholarly endeavour. This owed much to the efforts the Frankish ruler devoted to the promotion of arts, education, and scholarship. It is often referred to as the Carolingian Renaissance, even if there are few modern scholars who find the term 'renaissance' satisfactory. There was nevertheless an element of classical revival in the rediscovery and copying of important classical texts, such as Livy, Tacitus, and Terence. Astronomical and astrological texts were also copied, and illustrated with accomplished reproductions of late Roman miniatures. Even if there was no clear programme to preserve the classical heritage, much was preserved. Carolingian scholars showed an appreciation both of classical literature and, in the case of Theodulf of Orleans, of classical art. But this was incidental to their main concern, which, under prompting from Charlemagne, was the reformation of Christian society. They looked back to the Christian Roman past, exemplified by emperors such as Constantine and Theodosius and by popes such as Leo I and Gelasius. It was a past that seemed still to live in the churches of Rome, which provided the inspiration for Carolingian church building. The most ambitious building project of Charlemagne's reign was the palace complex at Aachen. The octagonal church still survives. It was modelled, fittingly, on San Vitale at Ravenna, from where some of the spoils used in the construction were obtained. Rome and Italy also provided Carolingian scholars with many of their manuscripts, Christian as well as classical.

The Carolingian Renaissance was not simply a matter of transferring what was left of late antique culture in Italy to the north; the Italian contribution was very important, but it was only one strand among many. Charlemagne attracted distinguished Italian scholars, such as Peter the Deacon and Paul the Lombard, to his court, where they found scholars and churchmen from Visigothic Spain, from

Ireland, and from Anglo-Saxon England. The conversion of Western Europe had produced a variety of Christian cultures, which developed in their own way. Britain and Ireland, for example, displayed a surprising precocity: in terms of education, scholarship and art they were in advance of the continent. The Carolingian Renaissance brought these strands together and synthesized them. It was not a spontaneous occurrence, but the product of Charlemagne's understanding of his moral responsibilities as ruler. These are clearly set out in the *Admonitio Generalis* of 789, which was addressed to the clergy of his kingdom. Charlemagne cited the example of King Josias, who called the Israelites to God by 'correction and admonition'. If the clergy were to carry out their duties properly, they had to be better educated so that they could instruct the people in the word of God. This message was reiterated a few years later in the 'On the cultivation of letters', which encouraged the setting up of cathedral and monastic schools.

It is clear that these exhortations had an effect. A network of schools, both cathedral and monastic, came into being. Not only did they produce a much better-educated clerical elite, but they also increased literacy among the aristocracy. The efforts of Charlemagne and his advisers to raise the level of education provided a foundation on which future generations were able to build. The Carolingian Renaissance did not peter out with the death of its originators, which happens frequently with cultural revivals, but made a lasting mark on the intellectual and cultural history of Western Europe, largely because it did so much to define its character. Once this had happened, Western culture became much less permeable and more discriminating in its reaction to outside influences.

Underlying the Carolingian Renaissance was a curriculum that owed much to the *Trivium* and the rhetorical traditions of classical antiquity, but was designed to provide a Christian education. Among the basic texts were works of Augustine, Boethius, Cassiodorus, and Isidore of Seville. But the feature that distanced Carolingian education most noticeably from the classical past was that Latin was now taught as a dead language, with a special pronunciation that differentiated it from the Vulgar Latin of everyday speech. This was to be an abiding aspect of Western medieval culture. It created an educated elite that operated in an artificial language. At the same time it gave a greater freedom for the development of vernacular literatures. It has been argued that the greatest work of Carolingian literature was the Old Saxon *Heliand*, which transforms the life of Christ into a Germanic epic in which the apostles become Christ's war band.

Much less exciting were the literary works produced at the Carolingian court, but they were more important for the ordering of a Christian society. Charlemagne desired uniformity of practice. To this end a request was made to Pope Hadrian I for a sacramentary, or service book. What Hadrian eventually sent was inadequate to the needs of the Frankish church, since it contained only the order of masses celebrated by the pope in person. It was left to Alcuin to create a satisfactory service book. Though others continued to circulate and to be copied, Alcuin's sacramentary brought some uniformity to the celebration of the liturgy. His work was to have a long future, since it provided the foundations for the modern missal. Another task on which Alcuin was engaged was producing a standard text of the Bible. Carolingian scholars also set about creating a standardized monastic rule based on that of St Benedict. Projects of this kind lay at the heart of the Carolingian Renaissance, and if they seem somewhat utilitarian, they had by-products that were more exciting. The standard of history writing, annals as well as histories, improved. There was a greater range of literature. Alcuin compiled a mirror of princes for Charlemagne. A couple of generations later Dhuoda, an aristocratic matron, produced a book of instruction for her son William. The intensity of the literary culture at the Carolingian court is apparent in the appearance of Carolingian minuscule at the end of the eighth century. Previously, manuscripts had been written in the impressive but laborious uncial. This was quickly replaced by the neat cursive of the Carolingian minuscule, which in the Italian Renaissance would be adapted as the most common typeface for printed books. It has often been said that the adoption of Carolingian minuscule had an effect not unlike the printing press, in the sense that it speeded up the process of copying manuscripts and produced a more utilitarian attitude towards the book.

The net effect of the Carolingian Renaissance was to raise Western culture to much the same level as that of Byzantium. To give one example, in 757 a Byzantine embassy brought an organ as a special gift for the Frankish king. It made a colossal impression. It emphasized the technological superiority of Byzantium. By 817 the Carolingian court had the resources to construct an organ without recourse to Byzantine aid. In some fields the Carolingians seem to have been well ahead of the Byzantines. There are a number of highly accomplished Carolingian ivories, which are not matched by the Byzantines until the tenth century. In metalwork Carolingian craftsmanship is seen at its most impressive in the bronze doors of the palace chapel at Aachen and at its most sumptuous in the Volvinio altar at St Ambrose's in Milan. Nothing like it survives from Byzantium. On the back are figures in cloissonné enamel, a technique that the Byzantines had to borrow from the West.

The Frankish histories of the time hint at Charlemagne's preoccupation with Byzantium. Pride in his Frankish ancestry and a deep sense of his responsibilities as a Christian ruler may well have been Charlemagne's main motivating forces, but he was also spurred on by a desire to emulate or to surpass Byzantium. The Second Council of Nicaea was decisive in this respect. It showed how little respect the Byzantines accorded the ruler of the Franks. As worrying was the doctrine that it was purveying. Its emphasis on images as essential to Christian worship offended the rather old-fashioned values that prevailed in the Frankish church. This did not mean that Carolingian art displayed iconoclast tendencies. There is much figurative art, but in a religious context it is mostly devoted to Old Testament figures and scenes, perhaps because, as we have argued, they were easier to justify. Carolingian artists were far more wary of an iconic rendering of New Testament figures and scenes, because this suggested that art could be infused with spiritual power.

Despite the condemnation of Second Nicaea at Frankfurt in 794, images remained an issue at the Carolingian court. Soon after Charlemagne's death in 814 the problem was reopened by Claudius, Bishop of Turin, who was an extreme iconoclast, opposed to virtually all accretions to Christian worship. He rejected devotion to the cross and to relics; he criticized the cult of saints and pilgrimage. His stand against images fortuitously acquired a special relevance when in 824 the Byzantine emperor Michael II (820–29) wrote to his colleague in the West, Louis the Pious. The tone was deferential, in itself evidence of the way the balance of power had changed. The letter contained official notification that the Byzantine church had rescinded Second Nicaea. It seems most unlikely that it was drawn up expressly to appeal to Frankish susceptibilities. If it was, then it was done most cunningly. The Byzantine emperor showed how image veneration meant that crosses were expelled from the churches. He drew attention to aberrations, such as images standing in as godparents, or paints scraped from icons being mixed with the communion elements, or even icons serving as altars. These were iconoclast horror stories, but they struck a chord at the Carolingian court. Louis the Pious ordered a reasoned response, which took the form of a document known as the *Libellus synodalis*. It was presented to a synod that met at Paris in 825. It recorded Frankish opposition to the veneration of images and it criticized Pope Hadrian I for his support of the Second Council of Nicaea. While refusing to countenance the extreme iconoclasm of Claudius of Turin, the more subtle iconoclasm of Agobard, Bishop of Lyons, reflected the mood of the Carolingian court. Its foundation was Augustine's argument that only Christ mediates between God and man. Images could not be allowed to usurp the role of Christ, for this would imply the superiority of matter over the spirit. Agobard accepted that images might serve as memorials, so he approved of images of the councils because these were memorials of orthodox faith. Even if the Caroline Books did not circulate widely, it was their line of thought that prevailed among Carolingian intellectuals. Hrabanus Maurus, Abbot of Fulda and later Archbishop of Mainz, gave it as his opinion that 'the written word is the perfect and blessed norm of salvation, while painting may delight the gaze, when it is new, but, when it is old, it is a burden, for it vanishes fast and is not a faithful transmitter of truth'. Walahfrid Strabo accepted historical images and admitted that they were conducive to pious thoughts, but maintained that to venerate them was pure superstition. None of these Carolingian churchmen had any difficulty in accepting the idea of images as the books of the illiterate.

The Carolingian reaction to Second Nicaea helped to give definition to the civilization of Western Christendom, which to that point had been both fragmented and curiously out of focus. It instilled a particular view of the purposes of religious art, which was to be subordinated where possible to the written word, so that there are those strange Carolingian images made up of words. Historical images and narrative scenes were acceptable. It was the image as icon that was the object of deep distrust. Images were not be venerated. There was a refusal to concede that they could act as the focus of spiritual forces.

This distrust of the icon marked an important difference between the West and Byzantium, and had a quite unexpected consequence. While little or no free-standing statuary survives from medieval Byzantium, it is one of the glories of medieval art in the West. The explanation for this lies paradoxically in the suspicion there was of the icon in the West and in the corresponding willingness to venerate relics. Increasingly, these would be housed in reliquaries that took the form of statues of the saint. It was a practice that aroused the disapproval of learned clerics, such as Bernard of Angers. But he soon repented of the scorn he had heaped on the statue-reliquary of Sainte-Foy at Conques when he learnt of the miracles that had been worked at her shrine. He realized that it was not 'a pagan idol to which sacrifices were made nor an object of divination, but the pious memorial of a Virgin saint before whom the faithful find the compunction which makes them implore her intercession for their sins'. The popularity in the West of the statue-reliquary provides just one example of the various artistic forms that piety took. It underlines how different in this regard the West was from Byzantium.

Chapter Seven

THE TRIUMPH OF ORTHODOXY

Charlemagne's imperial coronation on Christmas Day 800 turned out to be less of a humiliation than many at Byzantium anticipated. At the end of his reign Charlemagne conceded that only the Byzantine emperor had the right to be called Emperor of the Romans. This safeguarded the Byzantine claim to be the continuation of the Roman Empire. Even so, the Byzantines were reminded of the limitations of their effective power. The swift and nearly total triumph of Islam had a traumatic impact on Byzantium. The immediate reaction had been apocalyptical: Islam seemed to portend the beginning of the end of the world. This proved not to be the case, but Byzantium's imperial claims seemed unrealistic when placed alongside the might of Islam. They were kept alive by the notion that territorial losses counted for little beside the fact of Constantinople's divinely ordained survival. This was the core of the Byzantine identity, but it had been severely tested by pressure from Islam. It needed to be redefined. The iconoclasts sought to do this in traditional fashion around the emperor and the hierarchy of the church. They rejected veneration of images as an unnecessary innovation, which in some cases spilled over into idolatry. Their opponents insisted that orthodoxy alone was a sufficient basis for a Byzantine identity. Orthodoxy soon came to be equated with the defence of images and was a shorthand for the pre-dominance of a spiritual elite. But opposition to iconoclasm had next to no support from either the episcopal bench or the populace of Constantinople. At its heart was a monastic caucus. Its strength derived from its many adherents in the higher ranks of the administration, who, among other things, will have seen that images no longer constituted any kind of danger now that order had been restored to Byzantine society through the reassertion of imperial authority. The very reverse: images could be used to extol imperial authority and to present Constantinople as the new Sion.

THE IMAGE TRIUMPHANT

Emperor Theophilos seemed to contain opposition to his regime without much difficulty, yet within scarcely a year of his death iconoclasm was discarded and the return of images was celebrated on 11 March 843 as the Triumph of Orthodoxy. As we have seen, this was the work of his widow, Theodora, and a clique composed of her relatives and supporters, who organized a council to restore images in conformity with the Second Council of Nicaea. Their motivation remains obscure. Empress Theodora was in a weak position as regent for her three-year-old son, Michael III. Theophilos's reign had ended in a series of defeats at the hands of the caliphate and a humiliating appeal to the Frankish emperor for military aid. These failures, no doubt, helped to discredit iconoclasm.

There are similarities with the restoration of images by Empress Irene in 787. The intention was to bring peace and harmony to Byzantine society. Irene entrusted the task to the patriarch Tarasius, an ex-civil servant; Theodora chose as her patriarch Methodius (843–7). It is true that he was a monk, but he had also become a prominent figure at court under Theophilos. It may well have been under his guidance that Theodora decided on the restoration of images as the best way of effecting a reconciliation between the different sections of society. Methodius aimed to mollify the monastic wing by appointing Michael, a prominent monastic opponent of Theophilos, as his *synkellos*, or spiritual adviser. Methodius's approach was a gradualist one, just as Tarasios's had been. In exactly the same way, it earned him the enmity of the Studites, the followers of Theodore of Stoudios, who feared a loss of influence should the restoration of images be carried out under patriarchal auspices.

No more than the previous restoration of images did the Triumph of Orthodoxy immediately heal the divisions among Byzantium's elite. When Methodius died in 847 he was succeeded by Ignatius (847–58), a son of the iconophile emperor Michael I (811–13). The new patriarch succeeded in placating the Studites, but only at the expense of infuriating Methodius's supporters. These included Theodora's brother, Caesar Bardas, who was becoming increasingly powerful as his nephew, Michael III, grew up and became resentful of his mother's influence. While in no way an iconoclast sympathizer, Caesar Bardas was a patron of Leo the Philosopher, who had been the iconoclast archbishop of Thessaloniki and now taught at the palace school situated in the Magnaura complex. Caesar Bardas was not going to let the cultural achievements of the second period of iconoclasm disappear. His support for Leo the Philosopher only emphasizes the divisions there were among the elite. Bardas had Ignatius removed from the patriarchal throne in 858, replacing him with Photius (858–68, 877–86), a prominent civil servant. Already a renowned scholar, Photius's appointment to the patriarchate gave him the opportunity to dominate Byzantine cultural life. His intellectual pre-eminence did not endear him to the monastic circles that supported Ignatius. There was constant friction. Photius would be ousted as patriarch in 868, when Ignatius was restored. He then recovered the patriarchal throne on Ignatius's death in 877.

The restoration of images in 843 therefore ushered in a long period of division within the church. It raised the spectre of an iconoclast revival. Photius treated this as a real danger. In 861 he convened an anti-iconoclast council. This may have been a way of advertising his anti-iconoclast credentials: Photius seems to have been related to Patriarch Tarasius, while his father was exiled by Emperor Theophilos for his iconophile sympathies. Photius looked on the threat from iconoclasm from a viewpoint formed during his youth, when it was still a force to be reckoned with. In retrospect, it becomes clear that during the second phase of iconoclasm much of the heat had gone out of the controversy. Both sides were agreed that it was a matter of defining the limits of image veneration. In his letter to Louis the Pious, Michael II made it clear that he 'allowed those images that had been placed higher up to remain in place, so that painting might fulfil the purpose of writing'. For their part, the iconophiles accepted the ethical theory of images, which the iconoclasts had promoted. In the aftermath of the restoration of images the major division within the church, if not necessarily within society at large, was between a monastic clique that opposed concessions to the iconoclasts and a moderate group around Patriarch Methodius that sought reconciliation. The division was political rather than doctrinal. These circumstances help to explain the tentative nature of the restoration of images. One of the oddest things is the lack of icons – in the form of panel paintings – that survive from the immediate post-iconoclastic period. This may owe something to the accident of survival, but is more likely to be connected with a continuing suspicion of the magical properties that were once attributed to such icons. The evidence suggests that after 843 there was a marked degree of official control over religious art. It may be that the so-called 'Art Statute' of Second Nicaea was intended not to restrict artistic freedom, but to protect painters from the iconoclast charge that religious art was their invention, made for gain and therefore worthless. It seems clear that, whatever the intentions of the fathers of Second Nicaea, the 'Art Statute' was understood after 843 to mean that religious imagery had to conform with tradition. And, of course, the guardian and interpreter of orthodox tradition was the hierarchy of the church. In any case, virtually all the art that survives from the immediate aftermath of the Triumph of Orthodoxy is of official provenance, either imperial or patriarchal.

The iconography of the coinage was immediately changed. It reverted to the type introduced by Justinian II before iconoclasm, with Christ on the obverse and portraits of the emperors on the reverse. The only difference was that the legend identifying Christ as *Rex regnantium*, or King of kings, was omitted. This may have been a tacit admission that Byzantium had dropped its claims to universal authority. The iconoclast cross set up on the Chalke Gate, the ceremonial entrance to the Great Palace, was removed and replaced by an image of Christ. Within the imperial palace the Golden Banqueting Hall, the Chrysotriklinos, was refurbished. The image of Christ in the conch behind the imperial throne was restored. Facing it over the entrance to the hall was an icon of the Mother of God. In the vaults of the chamber were icons of angels, apostles, martyrs, and church fathers, with pride of place given to a joint portrait of Emperor Michael III and his patriarch. Slightly later, again within the palace, the Church of the Pharos was redecorated. In the dome, escorted by a choir of angels, was Christ Pantokrator – the Lord of All – his right hand raised in blessing and in his left, the gospels; in the apse was the Mother of God, 'reaching out her immaculate arms for our sake; obtaining salvation for the emperor and victories over his enemies'. In the upper vaults of the church there were again apostles, martyrs, prophets, and church fathers.

We owe this description of the Church of the Pharos to Patriarch Photius. In one way and another a great deal of the surviving art of the period can be connected with him. Photius was continuing work begun by Patriarch Methodius. For example, there is a debate as to whether the Khludov Psalter, one of the masterpieces of post-iconoclastic art, was done under the auspices of Methodius or under those of Photius. It is one of the marginal psalters, so called because they have marginal illustrations. Like those on most marginal psalters, the images on the Khludov Psalter were polemical in intent, directed against the enemies of the faith, most notably the defeated icono-clasts. Equally, the heroes of the faith are on display. The defence of images is represented as the work of Patriarch Nicephorus. Theodore of Stoudios makes no appearance. This suits those that urge the claims of Methodius as the inspiration behind the Khludov Psalter: Methodius was at loggerheads with the Studites, while Patriarch Nicephorus was his mentor. But Photius was equally devoted to the memory of Nicephorus. Although there is really no clear answer to which of the two patriarchs commissioned the psalter, Photius possessed one decisive advantage: he had so much more time than Methodius. He was also among the great intellects that Byzantium produced.

Photius came from one of those civil-service families that gave continuity and competence to the Byzantine central government. He had an excellent education, but we know nothing about its details. His *Bibliotheke*, or Library, summarized the reading of his youth. It was written while he was a member of an embassy to Baghdad and can be dated to either 838 or 845, when Photius would have been in his mid- to late twenties (the date of his birth cannot be established with any accuracy). Photius's *Bibliotheke* is a monument to voracious reading. His interest was in works of literature, history and rhetoric, both Christian and pagan; he ignored classical poetry and philosophy, though it is clear that he was acquainted with both. It was not exactly that he was suspicious of pagan texts, since so many feature in his *Bibliotheke*; it was more that the purpose of the work was to provide a guide to literary style that would satisfy Christian criteria. Photius aimed to establish an equivalence between literary qualities and moral and religious values. It was difficult to fit classical philosophy and poetry into such a framework since their values were so alien to those of Christianity. Though a work of his youth, Photius's *Bibliotheke* reveals his cast of mind. He was not interested in the classical past for its own sake. The past that interested him was late antiquity, the time of the first Christian Roman emperors, and he responded to the synthesis of Christianity and classicism achieved under them. It was the basis on which he hoped that Byzantine culture and identity might be rebuilt in the aftermath of iconoclasm.

Though enormously learned, Photius never held any formal teaching position. He was a civil servant; he became *protasekretis* or head of the imperial chancery, before his elevation to the patriarchal throne in 858. But he was at the centre of a literary salon, which used to meet at his house, and it was through this circle that he was able to mould the intellectual climate of his time. Something of its activities has been preserved in Photius's *Amphilochia*. This consists of a series of short chapters in which Photius replies to the queries of his friend Amphilochos, Bishop of Kyzikos. Most of these were of a theological nature, but Photius's answers reveal the breadth of his interests. Chapters 137–147, for instance, take the form of a commentary on Aristotle's *Categories*, which served as an introduction to logic. Photius approved of Aristotle the logician because his logic posed no obvious threat to Christianity. He was much harsher on Plato, whose ideal state and theory of ideas together represented a significant challenge to the Christian world-view. Photius denounced them as absurdities. He pointed to Julian the Apostate as an example of what happened when people took Plato seriously. Photius's conservatism emerges with some force from a sermon he preached on the birth of the Virgin. In it he ridicules those who scoff at the miracle of the virgin birth, yet are happy to accept pagan myths and metamorphoses. He had in mind those people who took their reading of the classics a little too much to heart and forgot that the true purpose of a classical education was to equip them to deal with the intellectual difficulties presented by Christianity.

Proper humility aside, Photius was well suited for the patriarchal office. We have already noted the stress he put on the threat from iconoclasm. There were family reasons for this, but that is not the whole explanation. The Triumph of Orthodoxy was hardly a reality. The ecclesiastical in-fighting delayed progress on the restoration of church decorations. The patriarchal Church of St Sophia was still untouched when Photius became patriarch. In his words it 'looked sad with its visual mysteries scraped off; it shed but faint rays from its face to visitors, and in this respect the countenance of Orthodoxy appeared gloomy.' Mosaics of the defenders of images – the patriarchs Germanos, Tarasius, Nicephorus and Methodius – were added in the patriarchal apartments. They might have been the work of Patriarch Ignatius, but Photius is a more likely candidate, given his ties to Tarasios, Nicephorus, and Methodius. Within the main body of the church Photius set up an image of the Virgin and Child in the apse. We know this from the sermon he delivered when it was consecrated on 29 March 867. It has long been assumed that the image that Photius was describing is the one that now occupies the apse of St Sophia. This has been questioned on good grounds. It has been suggested that the present mosaic was revealed only in the late fourteenth century, when an earthquake destroyed the image described by Photius, which overlay it. In any case, the surviving composition shows the Virgin enthroned, while Photius described the mosaic he was consecrating as showing 'the Virgin *standing* motionless before our eyes' [my italics]. The inscription that accompanies the mosaic runs as follows: 'The images which deceivers removed from here, pious rulers have set up once more.' The lettering is archaic and suits the eighth century rather better than the mid-ninth. This points to Irene and her son, Constantine VI, as the 'pious rulers' in question and the present mosaic as a prestige project carried out in the aftermath of the Council of 787, much like the replacement of the iconoclast cross over the Chalke Gate by an image of Christ. This raises many problems. The standing Virgin described by Photius would have looked much like the Virgin in the apse of the Church of the Dormition at Nicaea, which is known to have been restored in the aftermath of 843. It replaced an iconoclast cross, the outline of which could still be traced in the early 1900s. Replacing figurative images with crosses was almost standard procedure on the part of the iconoclasts, but even if the iconoclasts simply covered over the present apse mosaic in St Sophia, why did Photius not remove the whitewash and plaster? It is, after all, one of the supreme pieces of Byzantine art. It is also hard to imagine that the second phase of iconoclasm, a period of twenty-eight years, was long enough for such a mosaic to be forgotten. If there is to be an answer, however tentative, it may be that Photius wished to set his stamp on the Church of St Sophia and a new apse mosaic was his way of doing it. After 843 a standing Virgin, or Virgin Hodegetria, rather than an enthroned Virgin, came to be associated with the Triumph of Orthodoxy. Therefore, there is a distinct possibility that when we ponder Photius's sermon on the consecration of an image of the Virgin and Child in St Sophia, we should keep in our mind's eye a composition similar to the apse mosaic in the Church of the Dormition at Nicaea, rather than the present mosaic in St Sophia.

Photius emphasizes the lifelike qualities of the art. This was not just the mechanical application of Hellenistic norms of artistic judgement. To our eye Byzantine religious art is rarely if ever naturalistic. It is severe and formal. But Photius expected his audience to bring their imaginations and emotions into play, which would allow them to penetrate behind the figures portrayed in mosaic and to approach their reality. This will explain Photius's insistence that 'the comprehension that comes about through sight was far superior to the learning that penetrates through the ears'. In other words, art had a more immediate and lasting impact than the written word because sight was superior to hearing. The assumption was, of course, that books were read aloud. What the image of the Virgin taught were some of the fundamentals of the Christian faith: that she was 'an interceder for our salvation and a teacher of reverence to God, a grace of the eyes and a grace of the mind, carried by which the divine love in us is uplifted to the intelligible beauty of truth'.

Photius did not assume that it was an individual search, but a collective enterprise carried out within the framework of the liturgy. Equally, he thought in terms of a collective imagination, which is that much more impressionable than the individual imagination. Consciously or not, Photius did much to shape that collective imagination. He was most likely behind a ninth-century manuscript of the *Sacra Parallela* – a *florilegium* attributed to John of Damascus – which was decorated with no less than 1,658 marginal images. The great majority of these images are devoted to saints and Christian authors, including Patriarch Methodius, which points towards Photius as the mastermind. The project was on too vast a scale to be a private or monastic undertaking. It provided a portrait gallery, which, it was claimed, preserved the traditional iconography of the saints. Its literary equivalent was the tract by Ulpius (or Elpius) the Roman, entitled 'Concerning Bodily Characteristics', in which the features of Christ and a series of saints, apostles, prophets, and church fathers were set out. It was in this way that the artist was expected to conform to the traditions of the church. It was equally a means of shaping the expectations underlying the collective imagination.

We have already seen that a number of marginal psalters, of which the Khludov Psalter is the best known, were produced in the aftermath of the restoration of images and are likely to be connected with Patriarch Photius. The marginal images provide interpretations of the various verses. Their intention was not merely didactic; it was also polemic. Directed against the enemies of orthodoxy, they celebrated with some gusto the victory over the iconoclasts. It has been convincingly argued that underlying these images was a process of rediscovering the Byzantine identity, which had suffered during the iconoclast period. In the usual way, identity is most compellingly defined by negative means, by singling out enemies for vilification. Byzantium's traditional enemies had been heretics and Jews. Iconoclasm was presented as the culmination of the heresies that had threatened Byzantium. It could also be linked to the Jews. Photius was vehemently anti-Jewish and persecution of the Jews would be a feature of his second patriarchate. The reconstruction of the Byzantine identity was therefore done in a deliberately reactionary way, which continued to single out the Jews as the great enemy.

It had the advantage of reasserting Byzantine claims to be the new chosen people, but the reluctance of the marginal psalters to specify Islam as the enemy has always seemed puzzling. In the aftermath of iconoclasm Byzantine scholars sought to refute the strict monotheism of Islam on the basis of a study of the Koran, but they were not entirely successful. Islam remained a problem that Byzantium never solved. In a letter to the caliph an early tenth-century Byzantine patriarch claimed that Islam and Byzantium 'shone out together like two mighty beacons in the firmament'. This sounds like an exercise in evasion.

ART AND LITURGY

Images provided a positive affirmation of orthodoxy. Photius claimed the consecration of the image of the Virgin at St Sophia marked 'the beginning and day of orthodoxy'. But images were not to spin out of control, as they had threatened to before iconoclasm. Photius saw to it that they were integrated into the official life of the church. He refused to countenance the idea that an image somehow possessed magical properties. The power of the image increasingly lay in its association with the liturgy. Before iconoclasm there was no clear order to the decoration of a Byzantine church, but from the mid-ninth century standardized schemes of decoration make their appearance. Following the redecoration of the Church of the Pharos, Christ Pantokrator escorted by a choir of angels in the dome and a standing Virgin with her arms raised in the apse were to become two of the standard elements of Byzantine church decoration. They were complemented by a festival cycle containing the most important gospel scenes. These were missing in the Church of the Pharos, which suggests that the development of a standard scheme of decoration was still at an early stage. We cannot, of course, attribute its development exclusively to Photius, but he was clearly involved. The iconography was never rigid; there were always some variations. For example, the central dome was not invariably occupied by the figure of the Pantokrator. At the Church of the Holy Apostles at Constantinople, which was restored in the late ninth century, the central dome displayed the Ascension. Its message was slightly different from that conveyed by Christ Pantokrator, which emphasized divine control and order; the Ascension was more dramatic, since it provided a link between Christ's earthly ministry and his heavenly rule. It served as the culmination of the festival cycle, which celebrated Christ's life on earth. The new decoration of the Church of the Holy Apostles included such a cycle, one of the first Byzantine churches to do so.

The decorative scheme that evolved from the mid-ninth century was organically connected to architectural developments. The basilica was abandoned for centrally planned churches, which were united under a central cupola. Although there was some variety in the ground plan, this type of church is popularly referred to as the cross-in-square (or inscribed-cross) church. The experiments that created it pre-date iconoclasm, but it was only after 843 that the type was perfected. It is essentially, in the words of the great Austrian art historian Otto Demus, 'a conception expressed in the vaults', which build up to the central dome. The dome gives the illusion of a canopy suspended from heaven and matches the symbolism of the church building, which demanded that it be 'heaven on earth, a dwelling place for God, most high'. The new style of architecture also conformed to liturgical changes that had been taking place since before iconoclasm. The early liturgy was organized around a series of processions of clergy and laity into the main body of the church.

The basilica was the architectural form that accommodated this most effectively. As the procession became increasingly redundant, the sanctuary and apses became more clearly separated from the main body of the church under the enveloping dome, and the *templon*, or sanctuary barrier, more of a divide. The communion elements were now prepared in the northern apse rather than being solemnly processed into the church from outside. The liturgy became a drama performed by the clergy, much of it out of sight behind the sanctuary barrier, but the most important moments were witnessed by the laity assembled in the nave under the main dome, who thus participated in Christ's death, resurrection, and glory.

The meaning of this experience was heightened by the decoration. Again in the words of Otto Demus, 'The whole interior of the church becomes one vast icon framed by its walls.' This may well have been the most striking consequence of the victory over iconoclasm, but it meant that the response to the individual images would be guided and controlled by the liturgy. It was highly emotional. After all, the images helped the visualization not just of Christ's life and passion, but of the prophets who had foretold his coming, of the apostles who had believed in him, the evangelists who had spread his word, and the saints and martyrs who had been inspired by him. The subordination of images to the liturgy also guarded against the danger that images might become the focus of magical or superstitious practices. Whether this had been the intention of the fathers of Second Nicaea or not, the official church came to exercise a much more effective control over images than had been the case before iconoclasm.

The process of the restoration of images appears to have strengthened the Byzantine sense of order. It cannot all be attributed to Patriarch Photius, but surviving texts and monuments more often than not point in his direction. The critical period when information starts to become abundant coincides with Photius's first patriarchate. Photius was a traditionalist. He asserted that 'even the smallest neglect of the traditions leads to the complete contempt for dogma'. He presented his work as one of restoration. This is in the way of conservatives. The culture over which Photius presided was in many respects traditional, in the sense that it looked back to an idealized past. At the same time, elements borrowed from this past were rearranged to create something quite new. It was a process that had its own logic, but it was given clear definition by Photius's determination to safeguard the Triumph of Orthodoxy. The restoration of images was not of itself quite enough. Photius ascribed a central role to images in the worship of the orthodox church, but they were vulnerable unless they were fully absorbed into the traditions of the church. This meant their subordination to the liturgy and their control by the proper authorities.

THE MACEDONIAN RENAISSANCE

Photius did not look back just to an idealized past; he looked back to an imperial past, the past of Constantine and Justinian. As much as any Byzantine, he accepted that the emperor wielded divinely instituted authority. He was convinced that the health of the empire depended upon the piety of the emperor, that the empire was constantly renewed through imperial virtue. This did not mean that his relations with individual emperors were uniformly smooth. He was deposed from the patriarchate in 868 following the coup that brought Basil I, the founder of the Macedonian dynasty, to the throne. He was restored nine years later on the death of his rival, Ignatius, having recovered imperial favour through acting as tutor to Basil I's children. This does not seem to have endeared him to Basil's heir, Leo VI, who promptly dismissed Photius when he ascended the imperial throne in 886.

Photius was therefore fully conscious of the importance of imperial favour. The product of one of his most lavish acts of artistic patronage was an illustrated version of the Homilies of Gregory of

Nazianzus, now known as the Paris Gregory. Photius presented the manuscript to Basil I during his second patriarchate. The frontispiece shows Basil receiving a crown from the Angel Gabriel and the labarum from the Prophet Elijah. This is followed by a portrait of his empress, Eudocia, with their sons, Leo and Alexander. It is easy to understand why Photius chose the Homilies of Gregory of Nazianzos as a present for an emperor. Gregory was not only one of the great church fathers, he had also been appointed to the see of Constantinople by Theodosius I, who was remembered – sometimes conflated with his grandson Theodosius II – as one of the great Christian emperors of the new Rome. Photius deliberately played with the parallelism between Gregory and Theodosius and himself and Basil I. Together, Gregory and Theodosius could take credit for the victory over Arianism; Photius was offering Basil I similar recognition for the victory over iconoclasm. It was also a reminder that to fulfil their separate responsibilities emperor and patriarch had to work in concert.

Unlike the marginal psalters with which Photius has been associated, the Paris Gregory has full-page illustrations. Apart from the imperial portraits, their themes are mostly biblical, but there are some hagiographical and historical scenes thrown in. Part of their interest is the subtlety of their interpretation of the texts illustrated. This was Photius's contribution. The anonymous artist(s) provided the style, presumably with Photius's approval. The illustrations show the first clear signs of the illusionist style of painting, which was characteristic of the art associated with the court of the Macedonian emperors. Its masterpieces were the Leo Bible, the Paris Psalter, and the Joshua Roll, which can be assigned very roughly to the mid-tenth century. Their artists are steeped in the techniques of classical painting, to the extent that they make use of classical elements, such as personification.

The obvious debt of Byzantine painting of this period to classical art has led to the coining of the term, the 'Macedonian Renaissance'.

In the same way that 'Carolingian Renaissance' has proved so useful as a shorthand description of the cultural activities in the West in the late eighth and ninth centuries, so 'Macedonian Renaissance' has been used to describe Byzantine culture under the Macedonian dynasty, which lasted from the mid-ninth to the mid-eleventh century. 'Renaissance' is not, strictly speaking, the correct term for the cultural renewal that occurred from time to time in Byzantium and the medieval West. A great deal of ink has been spilt in the search for a better term, but to very little purpose. It is perhaps best to regard 'renaissance' as a rather flexible term, meaning no more than cultural renewal, which can take various forms. However, although connected by only the most tenuous links, the Carolingian and Macedonian renaissances have a surprising number of common features. They were both the product of a court elite and were, as a result, stamped with a certain artificiality; they were both designed to buttress the ideology of a Christian Roman Empire; they both looked back to the Christian empire created by Constantine, which they tried to recreate in idealized form; and under similar pressures both developed the more efficient minuscule in preference to the more cumbersome uncial script. There were differences, of course: the language for one; the city of Constantinople for another. Aachen simply did not compare with Constantinople, while papal Rome, which might have, never had a chance of becoming the Carolingian capital. There are three points to be made. First, the relationship of Carolingian emperor and pope was very different from that of Byzantine emperor and patriarch. Rome's distance from the centres of Carolingian power gave the popes an independence that the patriarchs never had, living as they did cheek by jowl with their emperors. The second point is that in the Carolingian West the educated elite was very largely clerical, whereas in Byzantium it was much more a lay phenomenon. Finally, the Carolingian empire was a more diffuse entity than the Byzantine, held together by a combination of respect for a dynasty and a sense of ethnicity. By contrast, in Byzantium the capital was the empire: power and resources were concentrated in Constantinople to an unprecedented degree. The significant history of Byzantium is, to a very large extent, the history of its capital. It was these differences that would shape the Carolingian and Macedonian cultural revivals and give them their distinctive character. Yet their shared purpose was to put the remnants of classical culture at the service of a Christian society and thus provide a new synthesis, which would justify the existence of a hierarchical order culminating in the imperial office.

There was, in other words, a strong political component to these renaissances. A taste for classical pastiche was a badge of the elite, perhaps more so in Byzantium than in the Carolingian West. Education always played an essential role in defining the Byzantine elite. This does not mean that illiterate adventurers, such as Basil I, were not able to penetrate its ranks and rise to the top, but it did mean that they almost always respected education and ensured that their children received the best. So Basil I entrusted the education of his sons to Photius.

The core of Byzantine education was provided by private schools. They offered a broad secondary education, which concentrated on what might broadly be termed grammar and aimed to provide a pupil with a mastery of literary Greek. Grammar schools would describe them more or less accurately. They were secular institutions; at this stage the Byzantine church had no special responsibility for education. These grammar schools were concentrated in Constantinople. There must have been some in provincial centres, though we do not hear of them. The normal pattern was for promising pupils to go to Constantinople in search of an education. The success of a school depended on the ability of the master to place his pupils in positions in the Byzantine administration, and the more successful grammar schools might receive some financial support from the patriarch or the emperor. The master's position at the centre of an old-boy network might give him real influence, so he made sure that he kept up with his prize pupils. The pupils of the same master formed cliques to help each other in their careers. The ties they formed during their school years were among the most enduring bonds uniting members of the Byzantine elite.

The grammar schools aimed largely at providing those going into the Byzantine civil service with the necessary education. Only a handful of pupils would proceed to higher education. There was no university education as such. Occasionally, the state would provide funds to support distinguished scholars capable of teaching at a higher level. The most ambitious project of this kind was undertaken by the emperor Constantine Porphyrogenitus (945–59), who established chairs of philosophy, rhetoric, geometry, and astronomy. He also provided bursaries for promising students and gave them dining rights on the imperial high table. The purpose of these measures was to improve the quality of those entering the civil service.

Funding education in this way was not entirely altruistic. Education and the knowledge it provided were valuable commodities in Byzantine society. They opened up the way to successful careers. They needed to be controlled. The new editions of classical texts that appeared with increasing frequency from the turn of the ninth century seemed to offer the educated man a vast range of knowledge and experience garnered by classical authors. This posed a threat to imperial authority, which rested on divine sanction but had little or no control over knowledge derived from the classical past. Political regimes have always found it expedient to control the past. This is what Constantine Porphyrogenitus sought to do by harnessing past experience to the needs of the imperial office. Under his guidance a team of scholars sifted through the corpus of ancient literature and docketed the information under a series of headings, such as 'Concerning plots' and 'Concerning embassies'. A vast encyclopedia, known as the *Excerpts*, running to some fifty-three volumes, was the result of this work. It was supposed to provide the emperor with a virtual monopoly of significant past experience, which it did so successfully, in fact, that all we have of some of the texts are the extracts in the *Excerpts*.

The most famous of the works compiled under the auspices of Constantine Porphyrogenitus was his Ceremonial Book, which contained the protocols for the most important court ceremonies of the imperial year. Ceremonial provided the core of official court culture at Byzantium. It gave meaning to what would otherwise have been a culture of extreme artificiality. Many of the most lavish works of art were produced with a ceremonial purpose in mind: the automata, for instance, which created such an impression on foreigners. In his preface to his Ceremonial Book Constantine Porphyrogenitus explained that he 'had made this compilation to display the imperial order at its most imperial and awe-inspiring'. He stressed the importance of ceremonial as a way of enacting the divinely instituted order that underlay the Byzantine Empire: 'Through praiseworthy order the imperial government is shown to be more majestic and attains to a greater elegance. As a result it is an object of wonder to both the barbarians and to our own people.' It was designed to make Byzantine superiority palpable. Liutprand, Bishop of Cremona, is a good witness. In 968 he was sent to Constantinople as ambassador by the German emperor Otto I. He wanted to take away with him some of the silks that did so much to enhance the glamour of Byzantine court ceremonial. His request was refused. He was told by an imperial spokesman that in the same way that the Byzantines 'surpassed all other nations in wealth and wisdom, so they had the right to surpass them in dress. Those who are unique in the grace of their virtue should also be unique in the beauty of their raiment.'

This virtue derived from orthodoxy, which was ideally maintained and protected through the agency of the emperor. There was a strong religious element to the ceremonial of the imperial court, with many of the major ceremonies taking the form of processions to the great shrines of the city. The most important was the patriarchal

Church of St Sophia, where the emperor received his coronation and where he went every Christmas Day to exchange the kiss of peace with the patriarch under its great dome. This event symbolized the continuing harmony between emperor and patriarch, which ideally ensured divine favour. The imperial palace was itself a major religious focus of Byzantium. This explains the care taken after 843 to restore old churches and chapels within its precincts. The most significant of these was Our Lady of the Pharos, which was a treasure house of relics, including nearly all the relics of the Passion. Relics enhanced Byzantium's claim to be the new Jerusalem, and, more than that, they placed the imperial palace and the imperial office at the heart of a conviction that Constantinople was a holy city. Never was this clearer than in 945 when Constantine Porphyrogenitus supervised the transfer of the Mandylion from Edessa to the imperial palace. One of the most sacred relics of Eastern Christendom, the Mandylion was a cloth magically imprinted with the Saviour's features, which, according to legend, had been sent by Christ himself to Abgar, the ruler of Edessa. The transfer of this relic was one of the great events of Constantine Porphyrogenitus's reign and confirmed his hold on imperial authority. An icon created to preserve the memory of the occasion showed King Abgar displaying the Mandylion. He was dressed in the imperial robes of a Byzantine emperor and his features showed a marked similarity to those of Constantine Porphyrogenitus.

CEREMONY, MONASTICISM, AND CONNOISSEURSHIP

Constantine Porphyrogenitus understood the importance of ceremonial and knew how to manipulate it for political and dynastic purposes. He created a new ceremony to celebrate the feast of Constantine the Great, long honoured as a saint. It entailed the Emperor processing from the palace to the imperial mausoleum at the Church of the Holy Apostles, where he was met by the patriarch.

The Emperor would first cense the tombs of his father, Leo VI, and of his grandfather, Basil I, with incense before praying at the tomb of Constantine the Great. It was a way of emphasizing the legitimacy of the Macedonian dynasty. Another side of imperial ceremonial was on display in the hippodrome, where the Emperor presided at the games. There he received the ritual acclamations of his people. Though reduced to ceremonial, it underlined the bond that united the Emperor with the people of New Rome. To a large extent, ceremonial served as a substitute for a political process at Byzantium. All societies make use of ritual and ceremonial, but rarely, if ever, have they been employed to such effect as at Byzantium. Elaborate ceremonial was a distinctive characteristic of official life and culture at Byzantium, far more so than in Islam or in the medieval West.

Ceremonial developed organically at Byzantium. Some of the protocols that Constantine Porphyrogenitus included in his Ceremonial Book went back to the sixth century, but a proper codification had to wait until the reign of Leo VI (886–912). This was symptomatic of the reassertion of imperial prestige in the aftermath of the defeat of iconoclasm. The emphasis was on the court hierarchy, the ranking of officers and dignitaries, and who sat where at state banquets. Ceremony uncovered the hierarchy that supported imperial authority. The codification of ceremony was of a piece with the encyclopedism of the Macedonian court, whatever form it might take: the official saints' lives compiled by Symeon Metaphrastes; the so-called *Menologion* of Basil II, which was intended as an official calendar of saints' days; Leo VI's military treatise known as the *Taktika*; Constantine Porphyrogenitus's *De Administrando Imperio* (a handbook of statecraft) or his *Excerpts*. The intention behind each of these works was the same: to provide a permanent foundation for the justification and exercise of imperial authority. They presupposed its immutability. This was wishful thinking. The Macedonian Renaissance did not put an end to cultural change at Byzantium, but it remained an ideal to which the late Byzantine Empire looked back with longing. The Macedonian Renaissance was a product of official culture and ensured that Byzantium did not display the cultural dynamism of either Islam or of the medieval West. Its public face was far too rigid and hidebound. Its official art remained turned towards the past.

There were, however, two distinct ways to escape from the conventionalities that threatened to fossilize Byzantine culture: the monastic ideal and connoisseurship. They may seem an odd pair, but together they gave Byzantine culture its distinctive flavour. Monasteries were the focus of aristocratic life. They served as family shrines. The elite found an outlet for their piety in the patronage of monasteries and holy men, and their prestige was fostered by backing the various currents of monastic reform that swept across the Byzantine Empire from time to time. In some cases it was aristocrats themselves who were the monastic reformers.

The restoration of images had taken place in such a way that the monastic church had been temporarily eclipsed, but thanks to aristocratic patronage it regained its wealth and influence. The monastic strand was always of the greatest importance to Byzantine culture. It was monasteries that initiated changes in liturgical observation and ensured that the icon remained central to Byzantine religiosity. Monasticism gave Byzantine culture a distinctive stamp. Its impact was all the greater because to a very large extent it remained outside the sphere of official culture.

The other escape for members of the educated elite was into connoisseurship, which often stemmed from a classical education. The antique statuary that still littered the public places of the capital continued to be appreciated for its naturalism. The devotion of some Byzantine courtiers to classical culture was so notorious that they were accused of pagan leanings. Such charges were the petty currency of court intrigues, but they had a foundation in the private cultivation of classical antiquity that went on among the educated elite. At the same time the Byzantines appreciated the Arab love for arabesque and abstract ornamentation. It was in this form that Islamic art made its greatest impact on Byzantine art. One of its attractions was that its meaning was entirely neutral but the skill of the workmanship was easy to appreciate. Even Emperor Constantine Porphyrogenitus was able to write in glowing terms about the craftsmanship of an Arab goblet that a friend had sent him. Connoisseurship of this kind linked the elites of Islam, Byzantium, and the medieval West. It was built around luxury objects: Islamic metalwork and rock crystal; enamels and ivories, which were common to both Byzantium and the West; silks, which could be either Byzantine or Islamic – experts find it very difficult to distinguish the one from the other. The taste was largely Islamic. It was but the faintest murmur of some continuing cultural unity.

The truth is that by the end of the ninth century Islam, Byzantium, and Latin Christendom had very little in common. They were divided in the first place by religion. Islam was uncompromisingly monotheistic and its adherents believed that they were in possession of the final revelation. The Byzantines saw themselves as the chosen people of the New Testament and were contemptuous of Latin Christianity, which in its turn was in the process of creating an identity around the papacy, the successor of St Peter. Islam created a network of cities stretching from Spain to China. It was an urban society, dominated by merchants. In contrast, Byzantium was a single city, which was more or less identical with the empire. We can see that its imperial claims were largely an illusion kept alive by a mastery of ceremonial and theatrical display. As yet, the West scarcely possessed a city worthy of the name. It remained an agrarian society, dominated by the warrior and the monk. Finally, each of the medieval civilizations evolved distinctive views on art for religious purposes, which serve as a touchstone of their differences. Islam rejected figurative art and employed calligraphy and abstract ornamentation in keeping with its austere monotheism. After the traumas of iconoclasm Byzantium remained true to the belief that the image could act as a spiritual medium, while the West emphasized its didactic function.

Chapter Eight

NORMAN SICILY:
AN EPILOGUE

B y the ninth century the process of separation was complete. Out of the ruins of the Roman world had emerged three quite distinct civilizations. All that was left of any sense of unity was an aristocratic taste for luxury objects. However, after centuries of being driven apart Islam, Byzantium, and the West suddenly found themselves brought together on the island of Sicily. This was the result of the conquest of the island by Norman adventurers in the later eleventh century. It was an experience that offers an interesting commentary on early medieval history and brings out exactly how distinctive Islam, Byzantium, and the West had become. Out of materials drawn from each of these cultures the Norman rulers of Sicily succeeded in fashioning their own style of life and culture, which modern taste has always found highly sympathetic. The Norman court created the illusion that it might be possible to recombine elements of the different medieval civilizations and produce a new cultural synthesis that would reunite the Mediterranean world. The reality was almost exactly the opposite: Islam, Byzantium, and the West were far too different for this to happen. The Mediterranean would remain divided.

THE BATTLE FOR SICILY

Sicily is the hub of the Mediterranean. Opposing cultures have always met there. By the eighth century BC there were Greek and Phoenician colonies. Rome's dogged struggle to secure control of the island from the Greeks and Carthaginians in the third century BC was not only testimony to its importance, but also the first and most significant step in its mastery of the Mediterranean. Similarly, the conquest of Sicily in 535 was vital to Justinian's plans to reconstitute the Roman Empire. While the Byzantines held Sicily their empire remained a Mediterranean power. Their stubborn resistance to the Arab advance across the island in the ninth century underlined how aware they were of its strategic importance. The Arabs started raiding Sicily in the late seventh century, but conquest did not begin in earnest until the early ninth century, when Palermo fell to them in 831. But it was not until 878 that they entered Syracuse, the Byzantine capital of the island. The Byzantines held on in southern Italy, where they made Bari their centre of power. They never gave up hope of recovering Sicily, even when their last bases on the island, such as Taormina, eventually fell to the Muslims one by one in the course of the tenth century.

By that time Sicily was firmly part of the Islamic world, and Palermo one of its great cities, as Ibn Hawkal's account of his visit there in the 970s makes plain. It boasted more mosques than any other Muslim city he knew – Ibn Hawkal was given a figure of over two hundred, and he could well believe it, because the local custom was for each family to have its own mosque. This custom could be taken to extreme lengths: the son of his host at Palermo insisted on having his own mosque. The city was certainly populous. Ibn Hawkal estimated the congregation of the Butchers' mosque at around 7,000. He observed that the congregation was made up of thirty-six lines of worshippers and that in each line there were roughly two hundred men. There are too many imponderables for us to extrapolate from this figure an estimate of the total population of Palermo, but given that the mosque served only one trade in one quarter of the city and given that there were five quarters, Ibn Hawkal's figure points to a sizeable population. He was impressed by the city's trade and by the fertility of the surrounding countryside, where new crops, such as rice and sugar, had been introduced by the new masters of the island. The wealth of Palermo derived in part from the natural resources of the island and in part from its position. It sat astride the main east–west axis of Mediterranean trade, now firmly under the control of Islam, and within easy reach of the caravan cities of North Africa, while to the north were the Italian trading cities, still in their infancy but capable of bringing to Palermo the raw materials that the West had to offer. The quarter that fronted the sea took its name, as-Saqalibah, from the Slav slaves, who were the West's main export to the lands of Islam.

The emir of Palermo had his own quarter of the city, which contained the palace, the prison, and the arsenal, but more often than not he was only the nominal ruler of Sicily. The island divided into a series of principalities, capable of combining in the face of an external threat, such as the concerted effort made by the Byzantines to recover the island in the early eleventh century. It was launched at the end of his reign by Basil II (976–1025) and was given up only in 1041. The Byzantines secured a bridgehead at Messina, but failed to break out. Their effort was in complete contrast to that of a small band of Norman adventurers, who, under their leader, Count Roger, seized the city in 1061. Two years later they won a great victory at Cerami over the forces of the emir of Palermo. In 1072 they entered Palermo in triumph. Local resistance would continue for another twenty years, but essentially it had taken a force numbering scarcely a thousand just ten years to conquer the island. It was astonishing, but it was astonishing that the Normans should be in Sicily, let alone wresting it from the grip of Islam.

Like other northerners, Normans originally arrived in southern

Italy as pilgrims, some going on to Jerusalem, some visiting the local shrine of St Michael, one of their favourite warrior saints, on Monte Gargano. A few stayed behind to take service either with the Lombard princes of Salerno and Capua or with the Byzantine viceroy at Bari. Their military prowess was appreciated; their rapacity less so, especially when their leaders started to operate on their own account. The most formidable was Robert Guiscard, one of a dozen Hauteville brothers who had set out from Normandy to make their fortunes in the south. They made the frontier fortress of Melfi the base for raiding Lombard and Byzantine territory alike, but it was nearby Benevento, supposedly under papal protection, that suffered most. Pope Leo IX (1048–54) organized an alliance against the Normans, only to be defeated and captured by them at the Battle of Civitate in the summer of 1053. This had all kinds of repercussions, but the most important was a reassessment of the Norman threat by the papacy. The denouement came in 1059 with the so-called Investiture of Melfi, where the new pope, Nicholas II, invested one Norman leader, Richard of Aversa, with the Lombard principality of Capua. Robert Guiscard, the other Norman leader, was granted the Byzantine territories of Apulia and Calabria and the Muslim island of Sicily. He had, of course, to conquer them first. In return for these grants, the Norman leaders promised to provide the military protection that the papacy was seeking. The architect of this papal volte-face was Desiderius, Abbot of Monte Cassino. He had been the first to see that there was much more to be gained from cooperating with the Normans than opposing them. It came in the first instance in the generous grants that his abbey received from the Norman leaders. The Abbey of Monte Cassino derived enormous prestige from its founder, St Benedict. It was not only extremely wealthy, but it was also the moral arbiter – or 'weather-vane', as it has been called – of southern Italian politics. Add to this papal blessing, and the Normans were turned from brigands into warriors for the faith. As a chronicler of Monte Cassino put it: 'Duke Robert

[Guiscard] repented of his past sins and guarded against present and future sins and thus he began to love the priests.' He had, in other words, become respectable. The cities of southern Italy that had shut their gates against him surrendered with surprising ease in the aftermath of the Investiture of Melfi, culminating with the surrender of the Byzantine capital of Bari in 1071. Robert Guiscard had entrusted the conquest of Sicily to his youngest brother, Count Roger, with, as we have seen, equally satisfactory results.

A COSMOPOLITAN CULTURE

Having secured southern Italy and Sicily with surprising ease, the Normans now had to organize their conquests. After the death of Robert Guiscard in 1085 the Normans looked as though they would fall prey to the factiousness that was an endemic feature of southern Italy. Guiscard's sons fought among themselves, but Count Roger, the conqueror of Sicily, was able to distance himself from these dynastic squabbles. He died in 1101, leaving two young sons, aged seven and five. This was normally a recipe for disaster, but Count Roger had done his work so well that his widow, Adelaide, seems to have had no trouble in safeguarding the rights of her children. It was the younger, also called Roger, who eventually succeeded. When he attained his majority in 1112, the occasion was celebrated by his knighting, which took place in the old palace of the emirs at Palermo. It was a momentous occasion for another reason too: it marked the transfer of Norman power in Sicily from Messina to Palermo, a step that Count Roger had been unwilling to take because Palermo was still a dangerously Muslim city. But, unlike his father, Roger II had grown up in Sicily. He almost certainly knew Greek and Arabic (his Greek signature was apparently more fluent than his Latin) and his clerks produced documents in Greek and Arabic as well as in Latin.

The population of Sicily was still largely Muslim, while the existing Greek communities were reinforced by immigration from the mainland, attracted by the opportunities that the Norman conquest opened up. The Greeks were strongest around Messina, which became very largely a Greek city. The Latin presence at this stage was restricted to French bishops and their clergy, who were put into the major sees, such as Messina and Catania, and a very few Norman families who had helped Count Roger to conquer the island. One of Roger's great strengths was that he took care not to dissipate his conquests by making generous grants to his companions in arms. This is in contrast to what happened on the mainland, where a number of turbulent dynasties – Norman and native – had established themselves. Because the Latin presence was so weak, Roger II really had no alternative – at least, in his early years – but to rule in Sicily in a style reminiscent of the Muslim emirs of Palermo. He has been called a 'baptized sultan': he took over the old palace and started to refurbish it, he kept the institution of the harem, and, like the emirs of Palermo, he interfered in the Muslim states of North Africa and brought many of their ports under his protection.

The basis of Roger II's administration was the *diwan*, which he inherited from the emirs of Palermo and which kept its records in Arabic and in Greek. These included boundary surveys, and lists of peasants and the taxes and services they owed. Roger II seems to have thoroughly overhauled the organization of the *diwan*. It is notable that he entrusted its running to Greeks rather than to Arabs, who seem to have held subordinate positions and were increasingly converts to Christianity. Arabs, whether converts or not, continued to dominate the palace, where the harem served as a form of household administration. At this stage Roger was tolerant of Islam. Many of his best soldiers were Muslims. He also favoured the Greeks and continued his father's policy of supporting the foundation of new Greek monasteries. For much of his reign his chief minister was George of Antioch, a Greek, originally from Antioch, who had served with the emir of Mahdiya before transferring to Roger II's service. He was a skilled naval commander, but was soon given general responsibility for running the administration. His seal reads: 'The Emir George, archon of archons'. He was also known as the emir of emirs. These titles somehow underline the cosmopolitan character of the royal administration. George of Antioch's monument is the Church of the Martorana in Palermo, more properly St Mary's of the Admiral, which he founded in 1143. It seems to have been intended as a family mausoleum. George and his wife, Irene, were buried in the narthex of the church. Although there are a few Muslim architectural features, the church conforms to Byzantine norms both in its planning and its decoration. George was able to hire his own team of mosaicists, who brought the latest styles and iconographies from Constantinople, such as the enthroned Pantokrator in the dome surrounded by four angels doing obeisance. George has left a portrait of himself prostrate at the feet of the Mother of God, who holds a plea addressed to Christ. It was probably placed in the inner narthex and balanced another panel, showing Roger II being crowned by Christ. Apart from the fact that Roger is designated *rex* and not *basileus*, this is a piece of Byzantine imperial art. It underlines that Roger's subjects tended to view his authority through the lens of their own tradition.

Roger nevertheless remained a good Catholic. The Catholic Church had a special claim on him. The legitimacy of his rule derived ultimately from the grant made by the papacy to his uncle Robert Guiscard at Melfi. This grant was the charter for the conquest of Sicily. It had been supplemented in 1098 by another papal concession, this time to his father, Count Roger, who was granted the right to act in place of a papal legate in his territories. Despite the exotic accoutrements of his rule, Roger II never forgot that his first loyalty was to the Catholic faith, the fount of his political legitimacy.

His loyalty was reinforced by events on the mainland. With the death in 1127 of Roger's cousin, William, Duke of Apulia, the direct line of Robert Guiscard died out. Roger was left heir to the Norman territories in southern Italy, which he set about securing in the face of local opposition. Behind the opposition was Pope Honorius II (1124–30), who feared an overmighty ruler on the threshold of Rome and was opposed to Roger's plans for his elevation to royal status. The Pope's death in 1130 allowed for compromise. The new pope, Anacletus II, (1130–38) granted Roger his request. On Christmas Day 1130 he was crowned and anointed king in the cathedral in Palermo according to Latin rite and with papal blessing.

Unfortunately, Anacletus was not the only pope at the time. It was a time of schism. Anacletus's rival, Innocent II (1130–43), emerged victorious and was not inclined to confirm Roger's royal status. His opposition involved Roger in a long – and eventually successful – struggle to obtain papal recognition of his coronation, which had the paradoxical effect of tying the new kingdom of Sicily even more closely to the papacy. Roger's coronation was an important event. It strengthened the Latin elements in his style of kingship. Roger and, to an extent, his successors were able to maintain a balance between the different elements that supported their rule, but there was now no doubt that Sicily was part of Western Christendom. The Greeks and Arabs slowly became less prominent at court and in the government of the kingdom.

The Norman court and government nevertheless retained its cosmopolitan character right down to the late twelfth century. It was a noted centre of translation from Greek and Arabic into Latin. Among the most important works translated was Ptolemy's *Almagest*. In his preface the anonymous Latin translator provides an account of the circumstances that allowed him to carry out the translation. He had been studying at the famous medical school at Salerno when he heard that a Sicilian ambassador had brought back from Constantinople a copy of the work. The ambassador was Henry, Archdeacon of Catania, whose enthusiasm for things Greek had earned him the nickname Aristippus, a character who appears in Plato's *Meno*. Henry was reluctant to hand over the manuscript to this eager medical student until the latter had prepared himself for the task of translation by studying Euclid and Proclus. Even then, the translator acknowledges the invaluable help of one Eugenius, 'a man most expert in the Greek and Arabic tongues, and by no means ignorant of the Latin'. Thus are we introduced to two of the most important translators at the Sicilian court: Henry Aristippus and the emir, Eugenius. Henry was a Latin; he was described as 'a man of the sweetest disposition, well versed in both Greek and Latin letters'. He was briefly chief minister in the 1160s, but it was not a happy appointment. He preferred his books. We learn that while on campaign with the king he began his translation of Plato's *Phaedo*. In the preface he outlined the Greek texts that were available for study in translation in Sicily: Hero's *Mechanics*, Euclid's *Optics*, Aristotle's *Analytica priora*. Henry also translated another Platonic dialogue, *Meno*. We learn from the preface that he was working on translations of the works of Gregory of Nazianzus and of Laertius Diogenes's *On the Lives of the Philosophers*.

Emir Eugenius was a Greek, one of those bureaucrats who served the Norman kings so faithfully. He translated Ptolemy's *Optics* from Arabic into Latin. He explained that he had chosen the Arabic version to translate rather than the Greek because the author's train of thought came through more clearly in the Arabic. Of his other translations perhaps the most interesting is that of *Stephanites and Ichnelates*. This was the Greek version of originally Indian animal tales. It centred on the Lion King and provided apt comment on court life. The translation of such a text pointed to close ties with the Byzantine court, because it had originally been produced for Emperor Alexius I Comnenus. These translations point to the similarities there were between the tastes of the Norman and Comnenian courts, so it is perhaps not so surprising that an illustrated version of Skylitzes's *History* – a Byzantine history covering the period 811–

1057 – was produced for the Norman court. The work is not translated, but the Greek hand points to a Sicilian provenance. The early illustrations are in a Byzantine style, but later ones show signs of Latin and Muslim influences. The illustrations depict not only events but also the rituals of the Byzantine court. It is a picture book that reflects a Norman fascination with Byzantium as a model to be emulated and surpassed.

There were also original works produced at the Norman court. Perhaps the most impressive was Idrisi's *Book of Roger*, which was an up-to-date gazetteer of the known world based on Ptolemy's *Geography*. Roger had the fruits of his work engraved on a silver planisphere. This provided a far more accurate map of the world than any of the contemporary *mappae mundi* then circulating in Western Europe. The Mediterranean lands and the Near East, as one might expect, are remarkably accurate. Idrisi was a Muslim who came from a family of Andalusian origin and was attracted, along with a handful of other Muslim scholars and poets, to Roger II's court, which still preserved a façade of Muslim culture. Roger had his own *'alamah*, or stamp, for authenticating Arab documents. He also carried a parasol. This was a gift from the Fatimid ruler of Egypt and was a recognition of his royal authority. In the fashion of a Muslim ruler he had attached to his harem a *tiraz*, or workshop, responsible for producing ceremonial robes for use at court. The most famous is Roger II's coronation cloak. It has a lion, the symbol of the house of Hauteville, savaging a camel.

ART AND ARCHITECTURE

The same cosmopolitan character evident in the intellectual interests of the Norman court emerges in its art and architecture. The Norman kings were all great patrons. They used their churches and palaces as a way of asserting their status and as a way of counteracting the criticism there was of Roger II's assumption of the royal title in

1130, which was seen by many of the rulers of the day as an act of usurpation. It is likely that it was at this time that Roger began the construction of a new royal palace. He had previously occupied the palace of the emirs of Palermo, which will have created the wrong impression. Roger's palace still exists, but apart from a single room decorated with mosaics, very little of the original survives, the great exception being the Capella Palatina. Its foundation charter dates from 1140, soon after Roger had obtained recognition of his royal title from Pope Innocent II. It was consecrated almost immediately, which suggest that building – perhaps for other purposes – was already well advanced. However, the mosaic decoration of the cupola was not finished until 1143, while that of the nave had to wait until the reign of William I (1154–66). Its interior is sumptuous and continues to excite modern admiration and enthusiasm. But it is a very strange hybrid. Tacked on to a nave apparently in the Western basilical tradition is a Byzantine cross-in-square church, which serves as the sanctuary. The Byzantine influence is emphasized by the mosaics, which are the work of masters from Constantinople. The scheme of decoration of the sanctuary more or less conforms to the Byzantine model, though a plethora of Christ Pantokrators – in the apse, in the dome, and in the lunette above the southern chapel – strikes a jarring note, at odds with the harmony of the Byzantine scheme. Yet another Pantokrator dominates the west end of the chapel. Despite the Byzantine workmanship the narrative scenes from Genesis and the New Testament that decorate the nave conform to Latin rather than Byzantine taste. But the Capella Palatina was not just a cross of Latin and Byzantine styles. There is also a strong Muslim admixture, evident in architectural features, such as the squinches that support the drum of the dome and the stilted arches. The decorative motifs that surround the marble cladding on the lower walls are Muslim too, while the honeycombed (*muqarnas*) ceiling over the nave is a major piece of Muslim princely art. Its surfaces are filled with depictions of the pleasures of Islamic court life: wine, women, and song. Though it is more or less impossible to make out these paintings with the naked eye, they are still a very strange decoration for a Christian place of worship. They would be just as out of place in a mosque.

They would be much better suited to the audience chamber of a Muslim ruler. It has therefore been urged that originally the Capella Palatina was a chapel in the Byzantine style at the east end and an audience chamber in the Muslim style at the west end. This seems a most unlikely solution. The combination of a chapel and an audience chamber would be almost sacrilegious. A more plausible explanation is that the Capella Palatina was originally planned as an audience hall that combined an entrance hall in Muslim fashion with a Byzantine throne room, such as the Chrysotriklinos at Constantinople. (The latter's plan, it will be remembered, was reminiscent of a Byzantine church. What is more, the imperial throne stood on a dais under a mosaic of Christ Pantokrator in the apse. This will explain the Pantokrator in the apse of the Capella Palatina.) However, once Roger had made his peace with Innocent II in 1139, it became politic to stress the Christian character of his rule, whence the conversion of a splendid audience hall into a palatine chapel. If this reconstruction of the early history of the Capella Palatina is correct, it will help to explain why it displays such an eye-catching fusion of Latin, Byzantine, and Muslim elements. It works supremely well, but it did not lead anywhere. The Muslim element is difficult to find in the later ecclesiastical foundations of the Norman kings. This does not mean that the Muslim component disappeared, rather that it was limited to the Norman kings' private residences, such as La Zisa and La Cuba.

At the same time as Roger II was planning the Capella Palatina, he was also engaged on another foundation, the Cathedral of Cefalù. At some stage Roger may have contemplated moving his headquarters from Palermo along the coast to Cefalù. The importance he attached to it is clear from his decision to raise its church to episcopal status. The foundation stone was laid at Whitsun 1131 and building was completed in 1137, but not, it seems, in its present form. Roger II decided in the early 1140s that he wished to be buried at Cefalù and therefore started rebuilding. The eastern end was rebuilt on an imposing scale and shows marked affinities with the architectural styles of northern France, as do the twin towers of the west end. Sandwiched in between is a rather unimpressive nave, which may belong to the original building, since it is of local inspiration. The alterations that Roger II made to the architecture of the cathedral were intended to underline his French connections. However, the decoration of the sanctuary, completed in 1148, was done by Byzantine mosaicists. This was a tribute to the continuing prestige of Byzantine mosaic as an imperial medium, but the iconography was Latin. The apse is occupied by a vast and moving Christ Pantokrator. In the lower registers stands the Mother of God flanked by angels and below her the apostles. On the side walls was depicted the lineage that linked Old Testament prophets and the fathers of the Church. The mosaics of the sanctuary provide the visual focus of the cathedral, but to a modern eye they seem out of place in a Latin setting.

Roger II had a porphyry sarcophagus set up in the cathedral prepared to receive his corpse, and another to serve as a cenotaph. In the end, he was buried in the cathedral at Palermo, where his porphyry tomb is still to be found along with a series of other porphyry tombs associated with the dynasty. It used to be thought that this use of porphyry tombs was just another instance of the Norman kings emulating Byzantine practice. If it was, they were looking back to an earlier period: the Byzantine emperors had long since ceased to be buried in porphyry tombs, because the material was so difficult to obtain now that it was no longer being quarried. It is more likely that the Norman kings were following the example of contemporary popes, who had themselves buried in reconditioned porphyry sarcophagi that had originally belonged to Roman emperors. It is a mystery from where the Norman kings obtained the porphyry for their tombs, but it is most likely to have been from Rome. Porphyry was so prized by the city-states of Italy, as a symbol of power, that there was an active market in porphyry centring on Rome.

It may be that Roger II's interment at Palermo was intended as a temporary measure, but the archbishops of Palermo were unwilling to lose so precious a relic. The cathedral itself in Roger's day seems to have been an old mosque converted to Christian worship. It was completely rebuilt in the 1170s by Archbishop Walter – something of his work can still be detected in the present cathedral – and provided a model for the Cathedral of Monreale, which King William II erected in the hills above Palermo. William originally founded the cathedral as a monastery in 1174, then had it raised to archiepiscopal status in 1183. Why he wanted another archiepiscopal see so close to his capital has never been satisfactorily explained. Royal pomp and prestige is only part of the answer. Monreale's endowment suggests something more. It consisted of large tracts of land cultivated by Muslims, while the diocese covered those parts of western Sicily where, even in the late twelfth century, Muslims continued to form the majority of the population. Monreale may, therefore, have been founded as a way of dealing with the Muslims by placing them under the supervision of the church. Its occupation in 1205 by rebellious Muslims suggests as much.

It was also a statement of royal power. William II invested huge resources in Monreale. By 1183 building was nearly complete. By 1186 the huge bronze doors – one of the great pieces of medieval metalwork – signed by Bonanno of Pisa were in place. By the time William II died, still a comparatively young man, in 1189 work on the Cathedral of Monreale must have been to all intents and purposes complete. It is on a vast scale: 355 feet long and 131 feet wide. Its planning is entirely Western, but its decoration was the work of Byzantine masters, except for the doors. It has been reckoned that the cathedral boasts roughly 82,00 square feet of mosaics, making it the greatest concentration of Byzantine mosaics there has ever been. However, the overall impression they make is most un-Byzantine.

The interior space of the building, dominated by a vast nave, has nothing Byzantine about it. There is no dome over the sanctuary crossing, just a rather crude Western lantern. The scheme of decoration, with its series of narrative scenes taken from Genesis and Christ's ministry, reflects Latin and not Byzantine taste. The apse is dominated by a colossus of a Christ Pantokrator with the Mother of God and angels below, as at Cefalù and most probably in the Capella Palatina. This had become a peculiarly Norman iconography. The Byzantine elements at Monreale were subordinated to the grim Latin architecture. The forbidding twin towers at the west end are a Norman feature. The sense that this is a Western cathedral is enhanced by the cloister, where the reliefs are in the style of southern France. Muslim influence is negligible, limited to the external decoration of the apse. Norman Sicily was being drawn inexorably into the orbit of Western Christendom.

INCOMPATIBILITIES

Muslim influences remained a part, but a strictly private part, of the court life of the Norman kings. Witness to this are the remains of the pleasure palaces of La Zisa and La Cuba. The first was planned by William I and completed by his son, William II, as an inscription in Arabic testifies. William II also had La Cuba built. It was finished in 1180, as, once again, an Arabic inscription declares. It lies at no very great distance from the royal palace, where, surrounded by water and parkland, it offered relief from the summer heat. The architecture and planning of these pleasure palaces represent a continuation of North African traditions of palace architecture. Both are on three floors and are of much the same size, but La Cuba is a rather simpler structure. Organized around a central domed audience chamber, which rises to the full height of the building, it was a place for festivities rather than a residence. La Zisa, which has survived better than La Cuba, is a more complicated building, with two focal points. On the ground floor, looking out through an arcade towards a basin with fountains, was a pump room, which still retains something of its mosaic decoration and which has a fountain as its central feature. The pump room served as an entrance hall. The main reception hall was a belvedere on the second floor, with a splendid view out across the city of Palermo to the sea. The central feature was once again a fountain. Arranged around these two halls was a warren of rooms, used as domestic quarters. There was no chapel within the palace, but one was built at a discrete distance to the west of it. This illustrates the separation that William II wished to preserve between his private life and the public face of the monarchy. The diverse cultural elements that Roger II seemed to be able to hold in balance were, by the reign of his grandson, separating.

This, at least, was the conclusion of Ibn Jubayr, a Muslim traveller from Andalusia, who was shipwrecked off Messina at the very end of 1184 on his return from pilgrimage to Mecca. His first impressions were favourable; they could have hardly been anything else, since he was saved from the shipwreck by the intervention of William II himself, who just happened to be visiting Messina. Ibn Jubayr made his way along the coast to Palermo, which reminded him not unfavourably of Cordoba. He noted that the city was encircled by the royal palaces, 'like pearls around a woman's neck'. The building that impressed him the most was the Church of the Martorana, which he visited during the Christmas festivities. It was in his opinion 'beyond dispute the most wonderful edifice in the world', and he was much taken by the columned belfry. The only mosque Ibn Jubayr describes was outside the city in one of the Muslim suburbs. It did not elicit quite the same enthusiastic response. The traveller noted that Muslims provided the city with its traders. They had their own qadi, or judge. They kept their mosques and came to prayers at the call of the muezzin, but were unable to congregate for the Friday service, since the *khutbah*, the Friday sermon, with its implications of Muslim political loyalties, was forbidden. Ibn Jubayr notes cryptically that ordinary Muslims 'do not mix with their brethren under infidel patronage, and enjoy no security for their goods, their women, or their children'. These 'brethren under infidel patronage' were almost certainly those of Muslim birth who had entered royal service, the price of which was conversion to Christianity. Ibn Jubayr tried to convince himself of the extent of continuing Muslim influence, so he drew attention to the way that the Christian women of the city followed Muslim fashions and went veiled. Apparently, in the royal household Frankish women had been known to convert secretly to Islam. Ibn Jubayr had heard that during an earthquake King William II found all his women and pages in their terror, invoking Allah and his Prophet, and he claimed that the King relied totally on the advice of his Arab eunuchs, even if for form's sake they had to renounce Islam. On his arrival in Sicily Ibn Jubayr was secretly interviewed by one of William's eunuch ministers, who derived great solace from the traveller's account of his pilgrimage to Mecca. The minister confessed that he had to conceal his faith. As some kind of consolation he sought out Muslim pilgrims, hoping to obtain their blessing and some memento of the holy places of Islam they had visited.

By the end of his stay in Sicily Ibn Jubayr could no longer deceive himself. He could see that the position of the Muslims on the island was deteriorating rapidly. William II insisted on the forced conversion of many of the leaders of the Muslim community, while there were all kinds of personal pressures on other Muslims to convert to Christianity. Ibn Jubayr's observations are borne out by the facts. From the end of Roger II's reign Arabs in royal service had been objects of suspicion, even if they had converted to Christianity. Philip of Mahdiya, one of Roger's most successful naval commanders, was of Muslim birth, but had converted when he entered royal service. Nonetheless, in 1153 he was arraigned on a charge of apostasy and burnt alive. It was an act that was out of keeping with Roger II's earlier toleration and appreciation of his Muslim servants. But Roger was now nearing the end of his life and the succession had to be secured. By sacrificing one of his Arab commanders in this way he could demonstrate that he 'was a most Christian and Catholic prince'. It was a reflection of the way in which the character of the Norman court was changing and the Latin element beginning to predominate. If Roger II hoped in this way to defuse prejudice against the Muslims, who were still a majority both in the island as a whole and in the palace, he failed. The assassination in 1160 of William I's chief minister, Maio, was accompanied by the massacre of the Muslim eunuchs of the palace by the conspirators, who were drawn from the Latin nobility. These acts were followed by the murder of Muslim merchants and traders who were going about their business in the city. Another group of conspirators fanned out into the centre of Sicily, which was being colonized by Italians from the north, and encouraged the northerners to massacre the local Muslims. 'Nothing could have been more welcome to them and they ruthlessly carried out their work' was the comment made by a contemporary historian. On the death of William II in 1189 the Muslim population rose in revolt. Their rebellion was put down with great brutality. The Muslims of Palermo judged it prudent to abandon the city and re-establish themselves in the south of the island around Agrigento. The death throes of this Muslim community would be completed some fifty years later, when Frederick II transferred its remnants to Lucera in southern Italy.

The Greeks did not come under such intense pressure as the Muslims. They retained important positions in the government until the end of Norman rule, but the spate of new Greek monastic foundations that had been a feature of the early twelfth century was not to be repeated. The clashes between Richard Coeur de Lion's crusaders and the Greek inhabitants of Messina emphasized the tensions that existed between Catholic and Orthodox, but the decline of the Greek community was slow and undramatic in comparison with that of the Muslim community. There were still educated Greeks in the thirteenth century, but their cultural and literary activities were now personal concerns rather than part of a court culture.

For a short while it seemed that the extraordinary circumstances of the Norman conquest of Sicily had reversed the flow of history, which had seen Byzantium, Islam, and the West drift further and further apart. Under the aegis of the Norman kings of Sicily, elements drawn from each seemed to recombine in a court culture of felicity and harmony. But this was an illusion. It soon became apparent that the divisions went so deep that it was impossible to preserve any balance. The Muslim and Byzantine elements were swept away before the Latin tide. Norman Sicily only confirmed the depth of the cultural and religious divisions that had been created in the early Middle Ages. It also pointed the way forward to Western domination of the Mediterranean.

GLOSSARY

apocrisarius	Papal representative at the Byzantine court.
apse	Semi-circular extension covered with a semi-dome, normally the eastern termination of a church.
Augusta	The honorific title of Byzantine empresses.
Basileus	The official title of the Byzantine emperors from the reign of Heraclius (610–41). It was introduced in order to emphasize the Christian, as opposed to military, origins of imperial authority.
basilica	A Roman hall, oblong in shape and normally terminating in an apse, which was taken over as the usual form of architecture for early Christian churches.
Chrysotriklinos	The main banqueting-cum-reception hall of the Great Palace of the emperors at Constantinople, the work of Justin II (565–78); imitated in the West.
diaconia	Charitable institution attached to certain early medieval churches at Rome.
diwan	Advisory council of a Muslim ruler adopted by

	the Norman kings of Sicily.
exarch/exarchate	Military governor/ship of Byzantium's western provinces with residence at Ravenna and Carthage, established in late sixth century.
florilegium	Anthology: compilation of extracts from other works devoted to a particular theme or subject.
khutbah	The Muslim Friday sermon normally delivered in the name of the caliph.
kastron	Byzantine fortress-cum-market town.
labarum	Constantine the Great's battle standard consisting of a cross surmounted by the chi-rho sign, signifying Christ.
mihrab	Central niche on wall of mosque facing Mecca.
menologion	A collection of saints' lives arranged according to the calendar date of their feast-days.
Monophysites	Adherents of a branch of the Christian Church that believed that the divine and human elements were united in Christ; mostly found in Egypt and Syria.
Monothelites	Adherents of the compromise formula that held that, while the divine and human natures of Christ remained separate, his will (*thelema*) and energy were one.
narthex	An antechamber at the western entrance of a church.
Nestorians	Adherents of a branch of the Christian Church that insisted on the complete separation of the divine and human natures of Christ, mostly found in central Asia in the Middle Ages.
Oikoumene	Originally the civilized world, but increasingly with a Christian connotation.
pallium	A mantle conferred on archbishops by pope or patriarch as a sign of office.

polis	Greek for city–state.
porphyry	An exceptionally hard purple stone mined in Egypt, which became a symbol of imperial authority.
qadi	A Muslim judge.
qibla	The direction of Mecca.
Renovatio	Political and cultural renewal under imperial and Christian auspices.
strategos	Byzantine military governor at the head of a theme (q.v.).
Taktikon	Byzantine administrative and military hand-book.
theme	Byzantine military province.
Theotokos	Literally, 'the Mother of God' – the usual Byzantine name for the Virgin Mary.

BIBLIOGRAPHY

GENERAL

Brown, P. *The Rise of Western Christendom*. Oxford: Blackwell, 1996

Cameron, A. *The Mediterranean World in Late Antiquity AD 395–600*. London: Routledge, 1993

Collins, R. *Early Medieval Europe 300–1000*. 2nd edn. Basingstoke: Macmillan, 1999

Fowden, G. *Empire to Commonwealth: Consequences of Monotheism in Late Antiquity*. Princeton, NJ: Princeton University Press, 1993

Herrin, J. *The Formation of Christendom*. Oxford: Blackwell, 1987

Mango, C. *Byzantium: The Empire of the New Rome*. London: Weidenfeld & Nicolson, 1980

Treadgold, W. *A History of the Byzantine State and Society*. Stanford, Calif.: Stanford University Press, 1997

EARLY BYZANTIUM

Cameron, A. *Circus Factions: Blues and Greens at Rome and Byzantium*. Oxford: Clarendon Press, 1976

Haldon, J. *Byzantium in the Seventh Century: The Transformation of a Culture*. Cambridge: CUP, 1990

Meyendorff, J. *Imperial Unity and Christian Divisions: The Church 450–680 A.D.* New York: St Vladimir's Seminary Press, 1989

Moorhead, J. *Justinian.* London: Longman, 1994

Norwich, J.J. *Byzantium: the Early Centuries.* Harmondsworth and New York: Viking, 1988

Norwich, J.J. *Byzantium: The Apogee.* Harmondsworth and New York: Viking, 1991

Treadgold, W. *The Byzantine Revival 780–842.* Stanford, Calif.: Stanford University Press, 1988

Whittow, M. *The Making of Orthodox Byzantium, 600–1025.* Basingstoke: Macmillan, 1996

EARLY BYZANTINE ART AND ARCHITECTURE

Belting, H. *Likeness and Presence: A History of the Image before the Era of Art.* Chicago: University of Chicago Press, 1994

Brubaker, L. *Vision and Meaning in Ninth-century Byzantium: Image as Exegesis in the Homilies of Gregory of Nazianzus.* Cambridge: CUP, 1999

Cormack, R. *Writing in Gold: Byzantine Society and its Icons.* London: George Philip, 1985

Corrigan, K. *Visual Polemics in the Ninth-century Byzantine Psalters.* Cambridge: CUP, 1992

Demus, O. *Byzantine Mosaic Decoration: Aspects of Monumental Art in Byzantium.* 2nd edn. London: Kegan and Paul, 1976

Elsner, J. *Art and the Roman Viewer: The Transformation of Art from the Pagan World to Christianity.* Cambridge: CUP, 1995

Grabar, A. *L'iconoclasme byzantin: le dossier archéologique.* 2nd edn. Paris: Flammarion,1984

Kartsonis, A. *Anastasis: The Making of an Image.* Princeton, NJ: Princeton University Press, 1986

Kitzinger, E. *Byzantine Art in the Making: Main Lines of Stylistic Development in Mediterranean Art Third–Seventh Century.*

Cambridge, Mass.: Harvard University Press, 1977

MacCormack, S.C. *Art and Ceremony in Late Antiquity.* Berkeley,
Los Angeles, and London: University of California Press, 1981

Mainstone, R.J. *Hagia Sophia. Architecture, Structure and Liturgy of
Justinian's Great Church.* London and New York: Thames and
Hudson, 1988

Mango, C. *Byzantine Architecture.* London: Faber & Faber, 1986

Mathews, T.F. *The Early Churches of Constantinople: Architecture and
Liturgy.* London and University Park, Pa.: Pennsylvania State
University Press, 1971

Mathews, T.F. *The Clash of Gods: A Reinterpretation of Early Christian
Art.* Princeton, NJ: Princeton University Press, 1993

Ousterhout, R. *Master Builders of Byzantium.* Princeton: Princeton
University Press, 1999

Rodley, L. *Byzantine Art and Architecture: An Introduction.*
Cambridge: CUP, 1994

Von Simson, O.G. *Sacred Fortress. Byzantine Art and Statecraft in
Ravenna.* Princeton, NJ: Princeton University Press, 1987

EARLY ISLAM

Cook, M. *Muhammad.* Oxford: OUP, 1983

Crone, P. *Slaves on Horseback: The Evolution of the Islamic Polity.*
Cambridge: CUP, 1980

Ettinghausen, R. and Grabar, O. *The Art and Architecture of Islam,
650–1250.* Harmondsworth and New York: Penguin, 1987

Grabar, O. *The Formation of Islamic Art.* New Haven, Conn.: Yale
University Press, 1973

Hawting, G.R. *The First Dynasty of Islam: The Umayyad Caliphate
A.D. 661–750.* London: Croom Helm, 1986

Hawting. G.R. *The Idea of Idolatry and the Emergence of Islam.*
Cambridge: CUP, 1999

Hillenbrand, R. *Islamic Architecture: Form, Function and Meaning.*
Edinburgh: Edinburgh University Press, 1994

Kennedy, H. *The Prophet and the Age of the Caliphates: The Islamic
Near East from the Sixth to the Eleventh Century.* London and New
York: Longman, 1986

Watt, W.M. *Muhammad's Mecca: History in the Quran.* Edinburgh:
Edinburgh University Press, 1988

THE EARLY MEDIEVAL WEST

Birch, D.J. *Pilgrimage to Rome in the Middle Ages.* Woodbridge,
Suffolk: Boydell, 1998

Brown, T.S. *Gentlemen and Officers: Imperial Administration and
Aristocratic Power in Byzantine Italy A.D. 554–800.* Rome: British
School at Rome, 1984

Bullough, D. *The Age of Charlemagne.* London: Paul Elek, 1965

Bullough, D. *Carolingian Revival.* Manchester: Manchester
University Press, 1991

Krautheimer, R. *Rome, Profile of a City, 312–1308.* Princeton, NJ:
Princeton University Press, 1980

Llewellyn, P. *Rome in the Dark Ages.* London: Faber & Faber,
1971

McKitterick, R. *Carolingian Culture: Emulation and Innovation.*
Cambridge: CUP, 1994

Noble, T.F.X. *The Republic of St Peter: The Birth of the Papal State
600–825.* Philadelphia: University of Pennsylvania Press, 1984

Ward Perkins, B. *From Classical Antiquity to the Middle Ages: Urban
Public Buildings in Northern and Central Italy A.D. 300–850.* Oxford:
OUP, 1984

Wickham, C. *Early Medieval Italy: Central Power and Local Society,
400–1000.* London: Macmillan, 1981

NORMAN SICILY

Borsook, E. *Messages in Mosaic: The Royal Programmes of Norman Sicily 1130–87*. Oxford University Press, 1990

Kitzinger, E. *The Mosaics of St. Mary's of the Admiral in Palermo.* Dumbarton Oaks Studies, XXVII. Washington D.C.: Dumbarton Oaks, 1990

Matthew, D.J.A. *The Norman Kingdom of Sicily.* Cambridge Medieval Textbooks. Cambridge: CUP, 1992

Norwich, J.J. *The Kingdom in the Sun.* London: Longman, 1970

Tronzo, W. *The Cultures of His Kingdom: Roger II and the Cappella Palatina in Palermo.* Princeton, NJ: Princeton University Press, 1997

INDEX